Asya's
Laws

Asya Rains

Asya's Laws

LESSONS IN LOVE
LOST AND FOUND

===

ASYA RAINES

AS TOLD TO CHARLES FLEETHAM

RIGHT BRAIN BOOKS, LLC
FARMINGTON HILLS, MICHIGAN

Published by Right Brain Books, LLC.
22000 Springbrook, Suite 106
Farmington Hills, MI 48336

Publisher's Cataloging-in-Publication Data
Raines, Asya, 1952-

Asya's Laws : Lessons in Love Lost and Found / Asya Raines as told to Charles Fleetham. — Farmington Hills, MI : Right Brain Books, 2006.

p. ; cm.
Includes bibliographical footnotes.
ISBN: 0-9763868-2-8
ISBN13: 978-0-9763868-2-7

1. Raines, Asya, 1952- 2. Latvians — Biography. 3. Latvians — United States — Biography. I. Fleetham, Charles. II. Title.

CT1234.5.R3 A3 2006
920 [B] — dc22   2005935770

Project production and coordination by Jenkins Group, Inc. • www.BookPublishing.com
Interior design by Debbie Sidman
Cover Design by Christian Fuenfhausen
Editing by Becky Chown

Printed in the United States of America
10 09 08 07 06 • 5 4 3 2 1

In memory of my mother, *Gusta Raines*,
and my father, *Kuse Raines*

For my dear children
Anna and *Simon*

Contents

Acknowledgments

My first and greatest appreciation goes to my dear friend, my first listener, and co-author of this book, Charles Fleetham. He opened the door to the exciting world of writing for me, and this story of my life emerged. Without him, *Asya's Laws* would have stayed a mere story, and I would never have dared to share it.

I would also like to express my special appreciation to the first readers of our book:

- Kathy Anderson for preparing this manuscript, for her support and help;
- Chelsea Fleetham for her youthful energy and encouragement;
- Teresa Weed Newman for feeling with me, for believing in my story, and for inspiring me through the journey of writing, from the first to the last page;
- Jo Anna Trierweiler for her interest in our book, her understanding, and for her positive emotional feedback.

Thank you to all our friends and family for the support they expressed while Charles and I worked on this book: Tanya Barg, Wendy Barrott, Valentina Borisenko, Rosa Fleetham, Anna Gluzman, Charlene Gronevelt, Gustav Grundman, Christina Kammuler, John Lydick, Jan Raines, Jeff Raleigh, Joey Silvian, Nina Tarley, Peter Tarley, and Vita Valetchikov.

Thank you to my new friends at the Jenkins Group for their project management assistance, book and cover design, and editorial guidance: Jerry Jenkins, Nikki Stahl and Leah Nicholson, and Rebecca Chown.

I would like to thank my best friend in Latvia, Ludmila Bagdasarova, for being a great part of my life there, for staying my best friend over the years and miles, and for making an incredible effort to read the English version of this manuscript.

I also need to thank my Latvian friends for their unflagging support and for the love I have always felt through the years of my life in Latvia and in America: Gera Brikman, Anna Brikman, Vija Garkalne, Inna Helman, Larry and Jane Beynart, Lilija Kalve, Natalija Krupnikov, Elena Palceva, Valentina Tserlyuk, Astrida Upite, Zhanna and Valdis Vismanis, and many others who don't yet know about this book but still remember me.

I would also like to give a special thank you to my relatives in Israel, Miriam and Aaron Rubin, for their support and help at all difficult and happy times.

Last, thank you everybody who will read our book!

By Asya Raines

Introduction

Dear Readers, this book is about love. It is for lovers, for sisters who have not spoken in five years, for daughters who can't make it through the day without calling their mothers, for fathers who have lost their sons, for cooks who remember the magic of the feast, for husbands who have not forgotten the power of gentle words, for sons who revere their mothers, for men who make wonderful soup for their wives, and for friends who still bring each other flowers.

I have told these stories about love to Charles Fleetham, my co-author. He helped me shape them into a book. As you read, you will find three languages: the language of love, my broken English, and the Midwestern voice of Charles, trained in creative writing at Michigan State University. I hope this mixture does not offend you. As you can understand, I wanted to make the language perfect for your eyes. But my friends told me many times, "Don't take away your own voice. The reader needs to hear it." I hope you share these feelings when you read my book as well as when you put it down.

Why am I writing this book? Very simply, to bring more love into the world. An ambitious goal for my Latvian heart, yes? I will tell you the source of this dream. Naturally, it is found in Latvia, in the capital city of Riga, my former home.

During a recent return to Riga, I visited the Museum of Occupation. This term doesn't refer only to the Nazi occupation during World War II; it also refers to the Soviet occupation that started in August of 1940 and continued, except for the years of the Nazi possession, until August 21, 1991.

As I walked through the museum one cold and gray December afternoon, reading about the many tragedies that occurred as a result of the Communist system, absorbing the sorrow and suffering behind a glass case, I saw a black and white picture of a group of young people being released from prison. When the Communists from the Soviet Union took the country in 1940, they freed these people on the first day of the invasion.

One of the people in the picture grabbed my eyes and I looked more closely. In the midst of the crowd, I saw my mother, my incredible Jewish Communist mother, with her firm, educated eyes and brave chin. I gasped. I stepped away from the glass case and put my hand over my mouth. Her face in this museum startled me.

Asya's mother, Gusta Jakobson. Photo courtesy of the Museum of the Occupation of Latvia.

For many days after this visit, the feeling of her worked through my mind. I was grateful and a little frightened by this flood of feelings. My mom died in 1997, but sometimes I talk to her still. I'm sure you understand. I told her how impressed I was with her role in the history of our country. In spite of the many troubles Communism produced, a pride surged through me, and I felt a need to share some of my mom's story with the world. I asked her what she thought, and in my mind I heard her say, "Asya, tell them how we have loved."

In this book, you will find a series of stories about my family and me. Most of the stories are set in Latvia, a land mostly forgotten by the world, except when it has been needed for an invasion. In America, I often hear that Eskimos have many words for snow. Did you know that Latvians have a thousand kinds of love? It is a well-known fact. In my stories, some kinds of love will be easily recognizable: romantic love, or the tender love of a parent caring for a child. Other times, the love will be harder to pick up and hold because it lives between betrayal and surrender or between courtesy and self-ishness. I am sorry for my teasing, but I must not let all my secrets out in this introduction.

Perhaps you would like an explanation of why I call this book *Asya's Laws*.[1] What does this title have to do with love? As you will see, my life has been a basket of decisions about love. To help with these trying judgments, most of which I made alone, I developed a set of laws. Dear Reader, I don't mean for these laws to be like medicine for your heart troubles! But, if even one law brings you more love, I will feel great happiness.

By now, I hope you are wondering about me. Am I an important person, or just a Latvian girl trying to get a little under your skin?

Allow me to take some weight off your shoulders. I am not so important that you must listen to me, nor I am such a nobody that you should toss me aside like old news. I have a college education, I speak three languages fluently, and I have the most perfect and wonderful children in the world.

Yes, as we say in Latvia, I am somebody with a pinch of pepper. Ask my warm friends in Riga and they will tell you this: "Only a girl like Asya would dare to tell you stories about the love that lives between a heartbeat and a bullet."

---

[1] Asya is pronounced "Ah-see-ah," with the accent on the first "Ah."

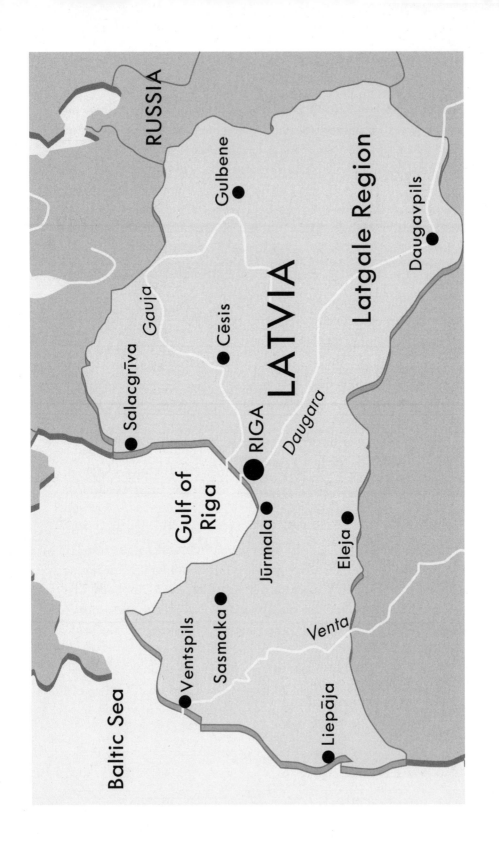

By Charles Fleetham

Preface

Asya Raines, who is the most consistently delightful person I have ever known, was born in 1952 in Riga, the capital and largest city in Latvia. She emigrated from Latvia to the United States in 1997. I helped her write this book because I fell in love with her story.

The idea for *Asya's Laws*, which covers the period in Asya's life from her early adulthood in Latvia to the second half of her life in the United States, came long before we decided to write this book, long before I had spent a suitcase of hours listening to her stories and trying to faithfully record their unique perspectives. In hindsight, I realize the idea was born the first time I met her and she told me she came to the U.S. for love. An hour later, after hearing only a few chapters of her irresistible story, I asked myself a fundamental American question: what makes this woman tick?

Asya was the second child in her family, three years younger than her brother, Jan. In 1952, the year of her birth, Latvia was occupied by the Soviet Union and ruled by the infamous dictator Josef Stalin. The map on the facing page shows Latvia on the eastern shore of the Baltic Sea.

Asya attended public school in Riga and graduated from the Latvian Technical University in 1975 with a degree in economics. She quickly entered the workforce as a software analyst for TransInform, a state-owned firm that produced management and accounting programs for transportation companies.

Her mother, Gusta Jakobson, and her father, Kuse Raines, were descended from a long line of Latvian Jewish families. They were both professors at the Latvian Technical University. Her mother taught the history of the Communist Party, and her father taught the economics of the chemical industry. They were both Communists. If you were raised like me in the era when "the only good Commie was a dead Commie," reading about Asya's parents will amaze you. They are so human! As Asya told me how the Communist system shaped her life, I must admit I felt a certain admiration for some of its elements and results. Again and again, as I heard her stories about her family and friends, I asked myself, how could the so-called "evil empire" produce such wise, generous, and courageous people?

As you will learn, Asya loves her parents. The American concept of establishing your identity by rebelling against your parents never occurred to her. When talking about them, she is never sarcastic, disconnected, alienated, or removed, and has never allocated one ounce of her suffering to the way they treated her. Not one ounce.

It is impossible to understand Asya without knowing a little about her country. Like Asya, Latvia is small, trim, and clever. It has about 2.2 million people, most of them well educated, yet it is no bigger than the state of Michigan, Asya's current home. Asya is cultured, multilingual, and industrious. So is Latvia. This mixture of European sophistication and emotional self-discipline is quite evident in Riga. Founded in the thirteenth century, Riga is the Paris of Eastern Europe. It is filled with museums, medieval churches, wonderful nineteenth century German buildings, coffee houses, and lively streets crowded with people speaking Russian, Latvian, and English.

Like Asya, Latvia has a personality four parts patience and one part insecurity. Latvia's overwhelming patience is due to long years of waiting and suffering for freedom and identity. Insecurity comes from being surrounded by more powerful neighbors—Russia, Sweden, Germany, and Poland—all of which have played dominating roles in shaping and ruling the land of the Balts, the name for the ancient tribes that settled Latvia in the ninth century. For Asya, insecurity seems to come from growing up a Jew in a country that, regardless of whether Soviets or Latvians were in charge, displayed an anti-Semitic shadow.

Latvians waited almost one thousand years, until 1918, before asserting their national independence, all the while preserving their language and culture. Not surprisingly, their independence was short-lived. The Soviet Union, always the larger neighbor, re-occupied the country in 1940 under the direction of Josef Stalin. It was then that Asya's mother, along with other Soviet sympathizers, was released from prison. Why was she a Soviet sympathizer? Quite simply, in the hopes that the Soviet system would be more fair to Jews than the Latvian government was.

Was Latvia invaded by the Soviets or were the Soviets invited? The argument persists to this day between Russians and Latvians. But, there is no argument that the Soviet Union exiled thousands of upper and middle class Latvians to Siberia, where most of them died in concentration camps.

Just as the Soviets were in the process of establishing their system in Latvia, the Nazis invaded in 1941, in violation of a secret treaty with the Soviet Union. Many Latvians danced in the streets and greeted the Nazis as liberators. They helped the Nazis eliminate Soviet sympathizers, and they helped the Nazis murder Jews. More than 70,000 Latvian Jews, almost 95% of the Jewish population, died in the Holocaust.

In 1944, the Red Army pushed the Nazis out of Latvia, but the Communist victory was not complete. Latvian freedom fighters took to the woods and fought the Communists for ten years before they were crushed. After World War II, the Soviet Union forced Latvia to accept the Communist system, as well as the Russian language, educational system, and culture. But, with its stores of patience, Latvia waited until the Soviet system crumbled and then regained its independence in 1991.

Today, Latvia is not only a member of the European Union, it is also a member of NATO, two facts that give you a glimpse of the drama that has played out throughout Eastern Europe. As we write, Latvia is generating a post-Communist boom with an entrepreneurial spirit second to none.

Even from this briefest of histories, one can sense the storms of suffering, flight, and revenge that have swept over this small land. To me, the Jews have had the toughest lot. Although Latvians and

Russians are remarkably different in culture, language, and religion, they have one thing in common—a strain of anti-Semitism. They both suppressed Jewish religious, cultural, economic, and educational aspirations to one degree or another for centuries.

Before World War II, if you were Jewish and lived in independent Latvia, what did you do when you were told you could only live in certain regions and that you couldn't go to the best schools? Naturally, you turned to the Soviets. When the Nazis invaded, where did you turn? Of course, again to the Soviets. But what did you do when the Soviet system your family supported prevailed, only to have Josef Stalin order the oppression of millions of Jews because he thought his Jewish doctors were trying to poison him?

In the 1960s, during the Brezhnev era, what did you do when you couldn't get a job, let alone a promotion, simply because you were Jewish? What did you do if you were a Jewish artist or scientist and you weren't allowed to leave the country, even to receive a reward honoring your contribution to your nation?

Finally, what did you do when the Latvians once again took over and overthrew the Communist system, the very thing your Jewish parents had sacrificed almost everything to build, knowing that the situation for Jews, though far from ideal, would probably now worsen?

Where did you turn indeed? Frankly, after learning the little I know about recent Latvian history, I am doubly grateful for my luck at being born and raised in the comfort of middle-class America.

As I said, I fell in love with Asya's story—not the story of Latvian independence or the fall of the Soviet Union or the story of Jewish courage. This is the story of a woman, and in the center of this woman is a personality. There are two kinds of people in the world, those with personality and those without. For those of you who have lived a few years, you know that having personality defies class, religion, achievement, and politics, even birth.

Asya is most definitely a personality.

Chapter One

Born for the Bed

You needn't be afraid of a barking dog,
but you should be afraid of a silent dog.

—Russian Proverb

My first true love arrived as it always does, without warning, no instruction, and no reason or rhyme. It was 1976, I was twenty-four, and I worked in a computer operations center at the Ministry of Transportation in Riga. For me, it was love at a glance. The first time Ivar walked into our office, with a swagger and shake of his blonde hair, I knew my heart would never be the same. I felt it in my chest. But don't ask me why I loved him. I don't know.

Looking back, I see that my love for Ivar was like a ship in full sail, much too easy for him to see from a distance. No wonder he stayed on the seashore, watching me go back and forth in the waves. But what did I know about love? In middle school, in high school, and even in college, true love came to everyone but me, and now that it was upon me, I was lost, which was why I was standing in front of Ivar's door.

It was a mistake for me to come, but I knocked anyway. I regretted it the moment I sent my shy tap tap into his home. He lived with his family on the outskirts of Riga in a nice home, and I had to make a long bus ride from the city to get there. I had no invitation to visit, no friendly "Come over my house sometime." My only protection was custom. In our country, it was a pleasant duty to visit co-workers at home when they were sick, even if they had only been absent for a couple of days.

Ivar smiled when he answered the door, a look that relieved me so much. He had been ill with heart problems. How could a young man, my Latvian man, have such a condition? I examined his face for signs of deeper feelings, for a line of rejection. There was nothing but a simple grin. And why not smile? On my good days, I owned a certain prettiness, a unique swishy swish of my hips that could make boys lean over to look at me.

The atmosphere at our workplace was good for falling in love. At that time, Latvia was part of the USSR, and Ivar and I both worked for TransInform. I was a systems analyst and he was an engineer, and our office was filled with idealistic young men and women practicing teamwork. "Teamwork?" you might ask. "In the Soviet Union?"

It is hard for Americans to believe that the Communist system was based on collective action and that we actually tried to put into operation those big ideas of equality and fraternity. However, don't mistake me or us. We didn't always like our system of government. Just as Americans are always talking about how their government is filled with liberals who take money from the rich and give it to the poor, we complained about party bosses who scraped away the riches for themselves. Yes, we had our just complaints, but after work we were just like everyone else. We played together, shared meals together, and went on vacations together. We were young and high tech, and we created some of the best software in the Soviet Union.

Ivar and I exchanged some talk about his illness and about work, and then he introduced me to his mom and his brothers. His mom made a striking impression on me that afternoon. I can still remember the smell of the gravy on her mashed potatoes and the warmth of the small smile of a woman who understands love and doesn't need to talk about it. As I sat and ate, I enjoyed being near her. She was the door to Ivar. I felt like I could belong to her, but I knew that she would never choose to open herself to me.

Why? Because I was a Jew whose family embraced the Russian culture and she was Latvian. Quite simply, we belonged to different cultures and religions. As I took the bus back to Riga, I thought about the challenge before me. Was it my challenge or hers? Even though I barely knew her, I feared problems. Some ethnic Latvians felt anger and suspicion toward Jews and Russians. This was natural but, to me, childlike.

To this day, I don't understand why people judge others based on skin color, size of nose, slant of eyes, or ancestry. For example, many Jews, like me, had black hair. Latvian men liked blondes. When Ivar returned to work, he told me that his brothers had teased him about my black hair. "Where is your black?" they had asked.

Political history made some of this distance and distrust on the part of ethnic Latvians. Large numbers of Jews, especially the educated class, had joined the Communist Party in the 1930s and had supported the Soviet invasion of Latvia in 1940. Here is why: before the invasion, the Latvians had forced many Jews into ghettos and had turned them into second-class citizens. The Communists promised to end this economic oppression and religious persecution that almost all European peoples inflicted upon Jews. It is easy to see why many Jews, like my mother, turned to the Communists.

On the other hand, those Russian Communists killed numerous Latvians when they took over the country, and many Latvians blamed the Jews for backing the Soviet takeover.

In the tradition of first true love, I swept aside any culture or history blocking Ivar from me. His mother might have this Latvian fear of Russians or distrust of Jews, but what could it matter to him? We had both been born after the war into a new and modern society. We were both educated in science and math. My formal education had been conducted in Russian and his in Latvian, but so what? I spoke Latvian fluently; I had learned it at home. Ivar had a similar ability to speak Russian, and he seemed to enjoy Russian culture. More importantly, we both liked blue jeans and the Beatles. As for religious differences, all the churches had been turned into museums and God had been buried alongside the Czars.

I had never even practiced the Jewish religion, though like my mom and dad I defined myself as Jewish. In Soviet times, when you turned sixteen and received your passport as a citizen of the USSR, you had to choose your nationality. Of course I chose to be Jewish, the only nationality in the USSR that was also a religion. Given my background, any other choice would have been difficult to explain to the authorities.

My nationality was written in my passport in black ink, in paragraph four. "Paragraph four" became a code for Jews. For example, if a Jewish friend was laid off or denied a promotion, we would ask, "Did it happen because of paragraph four?" Everyone knew what this meant.

When I came to the United States, I learned that it is hard for Americans to understand the difference between nationality and citizenship. For Americans, nationality *is* citizenship. When an American asks me, "What is your nationality?" I should answer that I am Latvian, because I'm a proud citizen of the Republic of Latvia. But I have difficulty saying this, because I am a Jew, born to Jewish parents.

I am not Russian either, because I was born in Latvia, though I grew up speaking Russian and embracing Russian culture, like many people raised in Soviet Latvia.

What is my nationality? In Soviet times it was Jewish and now it is Latvian, but in the distant future, I wish to be a citizen of the universe.

Despite my ingredients in this soup of Eastern European identity, I still assumed that Ivar and I would be able to overcome our differences. But just in case I had misjudged the amount of liberation in his spirit, I decided to embrace Latvian ways with a passion, and so I turned my Russian tongue and my Jewish soul towards Latvia.

I read books in Latvian instead of Russian. I spoke to Ivar only in Latvian. I even forced my Russian thoughts into Latvian. I dreamed of cooking delicious Latvian meals for Ivar like roast lamb with creamy potatoes. I wanted to melt myself into his world, into the smells of his mother's kitchen.

It wasn't that difficult for me to change. You already know there was a mixture in my soul. I was ready to be welcomed by Ivar and his mother, and there was not a single thought in my mind that Ivar would have to change for me to accept him.

Did my changes make any difference to Ivar? Not really. I had too much love for him and he didn't have enough for me. For this reason, Ivar moved in and out of my feelings. We would become close for a month, then we would not meet for two months, and then we would start talking again. The chemistry of love was not working! Did he have other women? I didn't know. Although I have since heard that silence is a source of great strength, with Ivar it was an irritation.

Do you know this rhythm? We danced with each other, but even when we kissed, I felt a distance in him. This made a big doubt in the back of my mind. Did Ivar refuse to commit to me because I wasn't Latvian, because I was too Russian? These questions I turned around and around until I decided I should find other inspirations.

One day at work, I saw a Yugoslavian tour advertised in our trade union brochure. All workers belonged to a trade union for a small fee that offered tours for very cheap prices. Like most citizens of the Soviet Union, I had never been abroad. I had been to Poland and East Germany, but we didn't consider the Soviet bloc countries to be abroad.

Yugoslavia was definitely abroad, and it was filled with exotic possibilities. Part of the West, even though it had a Communist boss, it had a reputation for social freedoms and fashionable clothes. I could already see myself in a pair of jeans, dancing in a jazz club with a dark European boy. But, to get to Yugoslavia, I had to pass an interview by the Old Veteran Bolshevik Committee. Can Americans imagine facing an interview by the local Democratic or Republican club to go to France, England, or Mexico?

Asya Raines, 1972

When this group of veterans called me on their red carpet, they asked questions like, "How will you explain that the economies of some of our republics are not as strong as the economy in Latvia?"

Wow! I didn't know what to say! All Comrade Asya wanted in Yugoslavia was sun at the beach, shopping, and just maybe to meet a handsome guy to replace her ache about Ivar!

A couple of weeks later, the trade union representative called me to her office and informed me that my application to visit Yugoslavia had been rejected, but then she said, "We still have some vacancies in the group going to Bulgaria. How about it?"

I was a little annoyed. I didn't want to go to Bulgaria. Known as the little brother of the USSR, Bulgaria actually tried to copy the Communist system as if it were the ideal. We knew better. Even though Bulgaria was an independent European country, we sarcastically called it the sixteenth republic of the Soviet Union.

"I wanted to go someplace truly different," I told Ivar at work when I expressed my unhappiness with the union's decision. "All they offer is Bulgaria."

"I am going to Bulgaria," he replied nonchalantly.

"Really? I will go as well!" I said, throwing Yugoslavia over my shoulder in a second. I noticed a flash of disappointment in his eyes, as though he were afraid I would hang all over him once we were there, but I did not care. I told myself optimistically, "We'll see." This is an example of a girl losing her mind. All I could imagine was the powerful chemistry we could make when we were far away from Riga.

It was now the summer of 1977, and our trip started with the expectation of friendship only. Ivar and I traveled with the trade union to a huge resort on the Black Sea. The first happy event occurred when I saw the resort. It was up to European standards, clean, modern, and smart. The last thing I wanted was two weeks in a Soviet resort. Imagine a housing project in a big American city, and you will see a hint of Soviet architecture, with little spark of beauty or individual personality.

My first task was to shop. I hopped and skipped to the market-place and found just what I wanted. They had Western clothes! With a smile so big, I bought a cute jean skirt that I wound like a candy wrapper around my waist. It was the first clothing I'd ever worn that made me feel like a woman of desire. In Latvia, I owned standard Soviet clothes. Ladies, think about buying all of your clothes off the rack and in a size that doesn't quite fit. Sometimes, it seemed I could have any color I wanted as long as it was gray. I was so happy in my skirt. Would my Latvian man notice my legs? When I ran into him in the hotel lobby, I probably made a pirouette.

"Wow! How much a skirt can change what a girl looks like," he exclaimed.

Did I hear a whistle in his throat? I am not sure, but the sight of me in a Western skirt instead of Soviet clothing changed his eyes for me. Magically, these two friends became a close couple. We rode bikes by the Black Sea, went to the beach every day, and ate delicious Bulgarian food. We even enjoyed fresh meat and vegetables, which were not as plentiful in the Soviet Union. I can still see the fresh tomatoes swimming in the sauces. We also went bowling, and I got to see my first jazz concert. My dream came true. Ivar and I danced together at the clubs and sipped strong coffee in the cafes.

My readers with Soviet blood may wonder how the KGB played their games with us on the trip. On the long train ride to Bulgaria, we tried to guess the face of the inevitable political correctness officer, and we discovered her identity soon enough. On our second day, in the hotel lobby, Ivar and I met a Bulgarian couple. We talked while drinking coffee, and they pleasantly surprised us by asking us to their home for dinner.

"Sure!" we said.

An hour later, one of the older women in our group informed me that she wanted to accompany us to the couple's home. Can you imagine? Everywhere you talked, somebody with big ears listened. She told me to call the couple and tell them to expect another guest. I felt embarrassed to make this call, but I had to do it. And so, the foursome became a fivesome. This woman must have been very bored listening to our conversation, for no one had any political thoughts by the Black Sea. She became a joke that Ivar and I bounced between us for the rest of the trip. You know what I mean—we found a way to always make a smile. We laughed about her hard job of pushing herself into everyone's lives.

Despite our best intentions, sooner or later every love story depends on luck or, as the Yiddish proverb says, "Better an ounce of luck than a pound of gold." In those times, unmarried men and women couldn't share a room, and the tour supervisor had assigned us roommates. But even the Communist Party, with all its power, was helpless against the forces of love.

One warm and sunny afternoon when the resort had turned quiet, I visited Ivar's room. His roommate had gone shopping. From this scene, you will quickly understand my attitude towards sex outside of marriage. If we liked each other, why not give pleasure to each other? Why do Americans make such a big deal about sex? They destroy the fun with their rules and their worries. Our bodies are made to give and receive this joy of touching. Even though I loved Ivar, I didn't expect him to make a lifetime commitment to me if we had sex. I was twenty-five, and I wanted to have this fun!

Ivar and I hoped for a long trip by his roommate. We started kissing. I gave him my inspiration and received his back. We moved our bodies together until a fire of love burned into us. When our clothes were about to fly off to the floor, the door suddenly opened. It was the roommate, returned from his shopping. Embarrassed, he quickly ducked into the bathroom. As we got off the bed, Ivar whispered to me, "You were born for the bed."

I often wondered what would have happened if his roommate had found his shopping more pleasurable, had taken a long, long walk along the Black Sea, or had slipped and broken his ankle. But luck was not with me that day.

After Ivar and I returned from the Black Sea, the blossom of our Bulgarian love slowly wilted and the distance between us returned. Then, Ivar left our office at the Ministry of Transportation. He didn't like working with computers or with women. He wanted to be outside, building roads and bridges. I invited him to coffee and dinner, but when we met, I didn't feel any inspiration from him. I felt stupid. Everything had gone so well in Bulgaria. I did not understand what wrong had been done, and he would not explain this return to his in-and-out dance.

My sad feelings were too personal to express to him. I wanted love to grow without a force of questions or accusations. I decided to bring the matter to a head, as Americans say it, by arranging to spend the night of my twenty-sixth birthday with him at his apartment. He had moved away from his mother's home, and I hoped that we still had the memories and urges of our unfinished love in Bulgaria. How could he refuse me?

I have two powerful memories of this birthday night. One, I was returning from a ski trip and Ivar picked me up at the airport. Because I wanted him so badly, I lied to my family. They wanted me to be with them on my birthday, but I told them I wanted to ski a little more.

When I saw Ivar in the airport lounge, I couldn't stop my smile or my mouth. I told him over and over of my happiness to be with him. He told me at least ten times to calm down, as if I were a child. My lie to my family turned into shame as we drove to his apartment. I still have not forgotten the patronizing tone in his voice. Oh that I could! Maybe then I could forget my second memory, his refusal later in the evening to make love to me.

"Don't you like me?" I asked him the next morning as we walked through Riga.

"No, it is not that. I do like you. I like everything about you."

"Then what is it?" I was asking him indirectly why he wouldn't love me like a man.

"I am afraid our relationship will become too deep," he said seriously.

"Why are you afraid?"

"I can't tell you."

"Do you have someone else?" I was willing to face an unhappy truth.

"No."

Relieved, I joked, "Do you have a little baby in Moscow?"

"No!"

"Then what is the truth?"

"I'll never tell you. Don't even ask."

I looked at him sharply. Suddenly, electricity poured through my body and I asked the question that crystallized up to my brain. "You don't want me because I am Jewish. That's it?"

"I am very afraid," he said, ending a long silence and all hope of love. "Maybe sometimes, in anger, in losing my self-control, I may say something about your nationality that would destroy our relationship."

I had always known the answer. I should have read this distrust in his face the first moment he saw me. It was his truth and I understood, but I was very sad. Not because I was a Jewish girl, and not because a Latvian boy rejected me. I was sad because I saw the roots of our ancestors attached to his heart, and neither life nor love could pry them out.

It was so ironic. I had been afraid he wouldn't accept the Russian part of me, but it was the Jewish part, the very part of myself that I had not fully embraced, that he could not accept. Asya's first law: love conquers nothing.

I left him, and the tears refused to stop.

Chapter Two

Remembering Makes the Treasure

Security is mostly a superstition...
Life is either a daring adventure or nothing.

—Helen Keller

T he best medicine in the world is a mother's under-standing. I carried my heart problem to her and she listened patiently to my long story of love lost. We sat together on her couch. Nearby was a weathered wooden desk, stacked with the books and papers of a dedicated teacher.

My mother had a gift for listening. She never filled the spaces between your words with her own thoughts. During World War II, she had learned that one mistaken word could mean life or death. Yet, despite all the troubles she had seen, when I think of her, I think of the quality of peace—plain, sweet, natural peace. She dressed in solids and pastels, the colors of calm rooms. She never wore any makeup. She never interrupted anyone, and she never raised her voice at me, not once. Really.

"I walked away from Ivar at the park without looking back. Crying, of course. And that's how it all ended up, Mom."

I loved her deeply. Her face had much sympathy for me. It was not classically beautiful, but the strength of her character made it so.

Gusta in Riga, 1946

Do you have this kind of feeling for your mother? She swept her hand across the side of my head. We had a relationship of strokes and caresses, not of laughing hugs and kisses. Those had come from my dad, a man who could make a good laugh. In that way he was very Russian, but my mom didn't have this Russian gene for joke telling. She was very accurate in her communication. Maybe this was why I had not confided in her much as a girl. Stories poured out of me like a waterfall, and I was self-conscious about overwhelming her patience.

"I know that your heart is in pain," she finally replied. "But maybe it is better like that. At least he was honest. You know, Asenka [this was her gentle nickname for me], life is never easy or simple."

My mother had come by herself to Riga when she was fourteen from Sasmaka, a village in rural Latvia. The sixth of seven children, her dad was a shoemaker who had struggled to put bread on the table for so many mouths. She had made her way to a friend of the family and had gone to work sewing clothes, not afraid to jump over the chasm.

I felt bad. At age fourteen, as now, I had been in my family's cocoon and had no thoughts of leaving. Now, I sat up to listen closely.

"Darling," my mother said, "you have heard much of my partisan story, but there is one more thing to tell. When I was a girl, any Latvian who wanted to really live came to Riga. It was 1934, and Karlis Ulmanis, the first Latvian president and our great Latvian father, had taken the political power into his hands." She put her sarcasm into *father*. "He chased out any progressive movement and turned towards fascists. Before the war I did not see much difference between him and Hitler." Then she added softly, "After the war, my eyes saw differently."

"Ulmanis was popular, especially with rural Latvians. Naturally, he did not favor Jews. Our people were not allowed into the best schools. Rich Jews sent their children to Paris or London. We were forced to live together in rundown neighborhoods. I saw the tides of this darkness and cast my fate with the Communists, who were coming from Russia to organize us. Asenka, you cannot understand the power of the party's pictures. By now, all have seen the warts. But before the war, our party spoke with passion about making a land of workers without racism or class oppression or hunger. I wanted this for Latvia so much, but human nature is not ready for it."

She continued, "As Hitler invaded Poland and the world started to burn in 1939, Ulmanis closed down our party. We protested in the streets and passed out literature about the revolution to come. We were arrested and sent to Central Prison."

Listening to my mother, I wondered if I had anything serious at all inside of me. A thousand questions could and should have been asked. Had my mom been scared? Had they tortured her in prison? What had it felt like to live in a cage? I couldn't imagine making this sacrifice for an idea. Yes, I lived in the Soviet Union, but I was no less a child of the '60s than any girl at Woodstock. I loved jeans, and nothing was better than a cute boy with long hair. As a young woman, my mom had loved Communism.

"What was it like to be in prison?" I asked courteously.

"I remember a group of young women who wanted a different future. We sang songs, talked incessantly. We made our plans. They didn't torture us, Asya. They weren't Germans."

"Thank God."

"After the party liberated the country in 1940, they freed us from prison and sent me to a youth camp west of Riga. There, I taught and worked with children. When the Nazis came in 1941, I helped evacuate the camp. We put the children onto trains. They were carried to the east. What could I do? Should I also leave for a safer place? Only one action seemed right to my ideas. I went to Riga and volunteered my services to the party. They made a quick decision of trust about me. Would I be interested in becoming a partisan? Yes. I wanted this chance. With no time for good-byes, they sent me deep into the country, past Moscow, where I learned to be a field nurse. They showed me how to clean wounds and set bones. Do you remember the surgical tools I have shown you? A razor and scissors."

My mind stopped at the familiar images of the razors and scissors and filled in this chapter of the story. My mom had fought in the woods for two years with the Soviet partisans, blowing up trucks, disrupting supply lines, and ambushing Nazis. For sure, it was special to me. My mom was a war hero. She had won the Red Star. It was a very high honor.

Then I thought about Mom's family. When the news came to Latvia that the Nazis were coming, everyone who could had fled to the east. My mom had three sisters and a brother who had managed to escape, but Mom's oldest brother had stayed with my grandparents in their village to help them. Did he know his fate before his decision? My grandfather had foot problems and couldn't run. They were simple country people. Where would they go? What would be left when they came back? Why would anyone want to kill a shoe-maker and his old wife?

When the Nazis marched into Sasmaka, nobody really knows what happened. Perhaps they rounded up my relations and the rest of the Jews in the area and took them to the woods and shot them. Perhaps they played soccer after they finished the murders. Nothing was found when Mom returned to Sasmaka.

By the end of December, 1941, the "final solution" for Latvia was practically achieved: out of the total of 75,000 Jews living in Latvia before the Nazi invasion, only 5,000 remained. By autumn of 1943, only 1,500 Jews were left. In my mom's family, three sisters and a brother survived. In the midst of the tragedy of the Holocaust, she felt lucky to have so many of her family alive.

"There was an Ivar, a Latvian, in my life during my war years," my mom said softly. She had my complete attention. I had always thought she had only loved one man, my father, who had died three years before.

"My partisan unit had a very young commander. His name was Anton. He came from Latgale. He was a very nice guy, with a beau-tiful smile and sparkling eyes. I was the only girl in the unit. Naturally, we came to like each other."

"Mom, it was probably more than that," I said.

She smiled softly. "As you understand, we did not have too much time for the romance. It was two and a half years of a very hard life full of fights, runs through the forests under the German's cross-fire, and caring for wounded friends."

I saw the sparkles of a young girl in her eyes.

"Yes, it was like a hell. We went on missions at night. If we were discovered, it meant certain death. For partisan Jews, it was even worse. They cut our insides out while we breathed."

"How could you stand this fear?" I asked. "I cannot believe your courage."

She waved away my compliment. "We did what we had to do. Nothing more. You have the same seeds in you. We snuck into our base camps in the day. We lived in holes, covered with leaves and branches. In the ground, we slept next to each other on beds made of birch. We took turns guarding our comrades until we woke up at night for the next operation. This was our life."

As I write today, I can see my mom's graceful face with the hidden smile in her eyes. She never told her stories in a tragic tone, but always in that very thoughtful way, sadly smiling and at the same time serious.

"Danger was in the camps, but we could run! I remember a winter when the woods filled with snow. The Germans started another attack against us. They knew our approximate location. As was their habit, they surrounded us in a quarter circle, opened fire in regular crossing patterns, and methodically moved to close the circle. The only way to survive was to run, to get out of that circle before the Germans killed us or locked it down and trapped us. We zigged and zagged through our well-known paths.

One of our guys was shot and couldn't run. Quickly, while the bullets flew, I threw a bandage on his wound, put him on pine branches, and pulled him with me. It was my job. He bled through the bandage and got cold. I covered him with the jacket I had been given by a nice lady farmer. It was a white rabbit fur jacket, warm and light. My poor boy told me to leave him, but I couldn't or wouldn't. Who knows the reasons? We ran for hours while the Germans chased us. I was very tired, but I didn't feel cold. We made it. We got through the ring of fire. But the boy died and my rabbit jacket stayed somewhere in the woods. It had fallen off during the chase. Isn't it strange that I still remember that jacket?"

I wondered, did my mom and Anton love each other openly, or did their love smolder over the two and a half years of combat? Did they break away into the woods for long talks and gentle touches? Sex was out of the question, but did they sleep next to each other for warmth? What did she really see in him? A future? Or a death with meaning? Did their comrades tease them? My mom was so intro-verted. I can see her blushing and turning away from any mention of her love. And, oh yes, I must admit that as soon as I learned about Anton, I started comparing him to Ivar.

"Asya, it is good that you have an optimistic nature," my mom said gently. I shrugged off her compliment. Whatever I was seemed unimportant in comparison to the suffering she had experienced.

"No, no, my dear. You are good. Very good. Always keep this confidence in love close to your heart. The romantic feelings between Anton and me certainly helped us to be optimistic, to believe in the future, to see a beautiful future after the war. This belief—so hard to hold in the middle of so much death and fear— saved a lot of people at the war from breaking apart psychologically. The vision of Anton and me together in Riga walking by the river kept me going through a lot of horrible nights." My mom had a far- away look in her eyes.

"As you can know by your own flesh and blood, we survived and made it through the entire occupation. This was no small achieve- ment, my darling. In October of 1944, the Red Army freed Latvia from the Nazi occupation. The war was over for the Soviet partisans. Also over was my romance with Anton. This ending was not as dra- matic as yours. We parted with his words that we did not have a future together. I was crushed, crushed, crushed.

"He left me because I was Jewish. Can you imagine that differ- ence being a problem after all we had been through? When we were at the war, it did not matter for him, or for any of our comrades, who I was, or who any of us were. Latvian, Russian, Jewish—we humans were all together, so tight together in such danger every minute of that long war. We did not think about such an insignificant detail as nationality. But after we escaped from the hell, everyone retreated to their homes, families, to the inhabited environments, to their nation- alities, to themselves.

"Anton was no exception. He went back to Latgale, his little home in soft and southern Latvia. If you think that his people hon- ored him as a hero, you are wrong. As you know, many Latvians hated our Soviet government and fought against it for many years after the war ended. So, the tables turned and Anton became the hunted instead of the hunter. Latvian freedom fighters formed their bands and went against our partisans, especially the Latvians who had fought with us, the very people who had helped free Latvia from Hitler. Did you know that the Latvian fighters fought in the woods until 1956, when we finally defeated them? As the saying goes, 'The scythe ran into the stone,' and Anton's own Latvians shot him in 1946. What a waste of life."

"A waste of love," I whispered.

"Only after I heard the news did I stop my wait for him," she said.

How many times have I come back in my thoughts to my mom's youth, to those years in the woods? Always, I compare myself with her: would I make the same sacrifice? Would I be brave enough? How would I handle those hard situations between life and death that she faced so many times?

I have not been brave enough to answer all those questions by myself. Nonetheless, whenever my life has led me towards new people and new relationships, I have come back to this deep and frank conversation, and my mom's story has helped me overcome many tests of love. Ivar was my first big one, and with her help, I passed it without anger or regrets.

"Isn't it ironic?" my mom said. "You and I were on the progressive side in these romances. We had the most to lose in these loves. You know how important it is for Jews to marry within the circle. Our Latvian loves had smaller visions of themselves, and now that I have you and your brother, I know that the disappointment was all for the best. And someday, if you don't make the mistake of trying to forget, you will see it the same way."

Then and now, when I remember my mother's words, I think of this law: remembering makes the treasure.

Chapter Three

My Mom Danced

All, everything that I understand, I understand only because I love.

—*Leo Tolstoy*

The story is told that a Roman matron once asked a famous rabbi, "How has your God been occupying his time since He finished the creation of the world?"

"He has been busy pairing couples," answered the Rabbi.

The matron was astonished. "Is that His trade? Even I can do that job. As many man-servants and maid-servants as I have, I can pair."

"Perhaps it is a simple matter in your eyes," replied the Rabbi. "For God, it is as intricate as parting the Red Sea."

After I lost Ivar, my family turned to matchmaking, that Jewish tradition of high honor. I had a large extended family in Riga, with many aunts, uncles, and cousins. My brother wasn't yet married, but my relatives didn't touch him. They put their matchmaking energy on me, the single girl in the family. My mother's sister, my aunt, arranged for me a parade of good Jewish boys, but I didn't like her interference one bit. I protested that I could find my own love, and I was a little bitch to those arranged boys. As we left our apartment to go on a date, I would typically announce, "I will go to this movie with you, but only this movie."

In August of 1979, after years of waiting, my aunt received permission to immigrate to Israel. Near the appointed day, my mom sent me to her apartment with a little going-away present, and there I encountered a man who had also been sent by his mother, another woman from Riga's Jewish circle, to deliver a similar package of good luck.

What do I remember of this life-making moment? His body was as tall as an apartment building in Riga. I was conscious of lifting my chin to see him. His face had a strong nose. He would not shake easily. His eyes were serious and wild at the same time. I needed a man who was not afraid to jump. He took me into his vision and crunched his eyebrows together as if studying me. In a matter of seconds, he made me feel like a book he had already opened and read the first two chapters of. I liked this feeling of being known quickly. We introduced ourselves and described our lives.

"I am a professor at the Latvian University," he said softly. "I am educated at Moscow University and carry a doctorate in psychology."

His accomplishment impressed me. How could it not? Moscow University was the Harvard of the Soviet Union. So, in this story, I will call him Professor. More importantly to me, underneath his credentials, I heard an elegant Russian tongue, with an appealing poetic flow and beat. Russians love a good poet, and I was no different. I wondered if he would read to me someday.

When the Professor called me the following day and asked for a date, I suspected my mom. Had she spun a web with my aunt and the Professor's mother? If she had, I didn't care, because the magic of old Jewish matchmaking had finally started working.

We went to a movie and then to his parent's apartment for wine and something else. Now that I am in America, I understand how much I was supposed to worry about giving myself to him on our first date, but in Latvia, I understood that I enjoyed being wanted, and whether or not he called me the next day was no issue.

The Professor called me the next day, the next, and the next. What a treat, after wrestling with Ivar's ghost of a desire, to be finally chased, to be explored in the grass at the edge of warm summer nights, by intelligent, sensitive hands.

We felt everything the same in our reactions—in watching movies and plays, in our tastes in cafes, and even towards life in Latvia. The Professor had no patience for the stupidities of the Soviet system or useless traditions. I couldn't imagine how he would put up with questions from the Old Veteran Bolshevik Committee. He was three years older than I and had been married once, and I could sense some of this experience in his touch. I must admit it to you, maybe I worshiped him a little. Ladies, you might have felt the same if he had read poetry to you. Sometimes he would call me late at night and read over the phone.

For one date, he brought a book of pictures from the London Art Gallery. He slowly paged through the galleries while I expressed my emotions and showed my thoughts. He watched me like what else—a psychologist. When we finished the book, he said, "This is so interesting. You have liked everything that I like." And so, the magical matchmaking trap closed even more in my heart.

Three weeks after our first date, he asked me to go on a camping trip to Greater Solovetsky Island.

"Solovetsky! We can't go without a group. You have permission?" I asked.

Situated in the western part of the White Sea, less than one hundred miles from the Polar Circle, Solovetsky is a group of large and small islands famous for their wildlife and medieval monasteries. The biggest island is Greater Solovetsky Island, and at that time it also housed a huge Stalinist gulag that had been turned into a museum. A former place of departure for political dissidents, some detainees were still kept there. For this reason, no one could visit without special authorization from the government.

"Don't worry," said the Professor. "We will find a way." His confidence won over my doubts, and I gave him one hundred rubles, about a month's wages. This was the last of my vacation money. I had recently returned from a wonderful two-week vacation at the

Black Sea with my co-worker Astrida, a trip that had completely relieved me of any remaining sad memories about Ivar.

The Professor was right, a way was discovered to get to Solovetsky, but it wasn't easy. At the district border town, I innocently bought tickets for a flight to the island, acting as if I naturally had the proper papers. During the trip, the pilot asked for them and we had to say, "We don't have any." I pleaded a long time and put on my sweetest face, so the pilot landed us on the island. There, more whining, all of it mine, was needed to get good documents for our visit. This was my first indication that the Professor was not always as good as his word. Still, what an adventure to be on Solovetsky!

We walked into the woods and pitched a tent and began exploring. We saw monastery buildings, fortress walls and towers, and the outside of Stalin's infamous gulag camp. We explored the island's inner lakes and the canal system between them. We saw stone labyrinths from prehistoric times, and from the shores of the White Sea we searched for beluga whales. Yes, the island was one adventure, but the bigger adventure was being so close to this man I hardly knew.

Not surprisingly, he discovered the first thing about me that he didn't like. We were on a trolley bus, and when I saw an old man standing up, I offered him my seat. This was a natural act of politeness, but for the rest of the ride, the Professor held up his nose and looked this way and that, refusing to speak to me.

"Why is he doing this?" I wondered. It was the first click of negativity in our relationship. Do you remember the first negative click in your most important relationship? Isn't it shocking? Everything up to now has been perfect, and suddenly you wonder if you have made the biggest mistake of your life. Asya's Law: never ignore the first click.

When we got off the trolley, the Professor berated me from the height of his personality and accomplishment. "Why were you polite to that man?" he finally demanded.

"What are you talking about?"

"Didn't you see how he treated people, how he barked at them, how he made everyone on the trolley uncomfortable? Everyone except you, it seems. You are too open to people. He did not deserve such courtesy from you."

"I did not see this man's rude behavior," I responded. "As you know, I was pushing to the front to get our tickets. When I got back to you, I only saw him standing. Is it wrong to be polite?"

"This man was bad."

"Would you have me be rude to everyone on the possibility that they will be discourteous?" I protested strongly, and the Professor saw his mistake. He apologized, and the click went away for the rest of our trip.

Because we were so close to the Arctic Circle, it never seemed to get dark. We didn't care; we had much to talk about in order to understand each other better. The Professor liked to test me with deep questions, and I remember one evening when he asked me where I learned how to love. I thought for much time.

"In communalka, where I grew up and where I still live," I finally replied.

He snorted. "Communalka" was our unhappy term for an apartment in which different families lived together. Let me take this wonderful word apart. Of course, "commun" means everything is common and is the root philosophy of Communism. "Alka" is a simple suffix added to "commun" that puts a sarcastic twist on this idea that strangers can live together in harmony without private ownership.

If you lived in communalka, you had separate living quarters but shared all common-use facilities—the kitchen, hallways, closets, and of course, the toilets. Anyone who lived that way remembers the combination of irony and sympathy they received when they told someone they lived in communalka.

This system started in Russia after the Great October Revolution in 1917, when millions of starving poor people were living in wretched conditions in wet and dark basements in big cities like Moscow and St. Petersburg. With encouragement from the Proletarian power in the Kremlin, many times from the end of a gun, rich, well-fed nobles divided their giant suites three, four, and even five times to give peasant people a warm and dry floor to sleep upon. As you can imagine, the world turned upside down.

Think about it, Dear Readers. Even if it is good to share with the less fortunate, how would you feel if, next Sunday, a family of six moved into your big house and you lost the ownership of all rooms but one?

"What good could come from communalka?" asked the Professor.

"It was not forced upon my family," I replied. "My mom willingly gave communalka. In return for her service as a partisan fighter, the party had given her the four-room apartment in which I live. You know there were very few women who received such a reward. She could have kept it all to herself, but she decided in the spirit of 'commun' to share it with people who didn't have a place to live. My aunt returned from evacuation in eastern Russia and my uncle returned from the army. Also, my aunt brought along a couple who had a daughter, and this eventually turned into a family of six. As my aunt liked to say, 'Better to live with a Jewish family than you don't know who.'

"It was the most crowded in my teenage years. Ten people occupied the same four rooms. My family—my mom, dad, my brother and I—had two rooms, and our neighbors—a grandfather, grandmother, mother, father, and two children, a boy and a girl—had the other two rooms."

I continued with my story. "My favorite was the old grandfather, German [pronounced Gear-man]. A quiet, tall, and skinny man, he seemed older than the oldest tree in Riga, and he treated me as his own granddaughter. He invited me into his room and talked to me and showed me mysterious postcards from abroad. Sometimes he gave me a jar of jam and said, 'Eat it; it's for you.'

"Dear Professor, you have been spoiled with your own apartment. Paint a picture in your mind of a line to enter the bathroom at seven each morning, ordered according to Communalka Rule #1: the one who gets up first goes to the bathroom first."

I laughed, and the Professor laughed with me. He had been raised in the luxury of a single-family apartment. Seeing a rare opportunity to educate him, I continued my lecture on communalka.

"Rule #2 was never to leave a wet towel on the floor. I often broke this rule. We never knew who informed on our infractions, but it was probably the next person in line who, upon tripping on my wet towels, shouted, 'Asya, you have broken Communalka Rule #2 again! With much politeness, I ask of you: please pick up your personal things.'

"Oh, well," I sighed, "there are so many memories from my teenage years. Living in communalka is a very strange experience. Of course, I would agree with you if you, with your Moscow education in psychology, would say, 'This is not a normal life. It is not healthy.'

"Yes, it was sometimes very irritating. The constant presence of non-family members in our apartment should have driven us crazy, but we learned to take it as a reality of our life. We joked constantly. We told funny stories about our lives to our friends. Most of them lived the same way. Some of them had four or five neighbors, so they also had something to tell and to laugh about. But there was no anger or hate. I have heard that some apartments lived in a hell. Neighbors fought and argued about whose turn it was to clean the floor in the kitchen, or about the electrical bills, or about scrubbing the bathroom. We did not do that. My parents would never have permitted it."

Today, there is something that touches my heart when I remember those years on the sixth floor of our elegant black apartment house. We never talked about it openly, but those neighbors became relatives of sorts. We cared about each other. We helped each other. I remember that whenever I was sick, their grandmother always gave me some tasty soup and asked if I needed anything, and our family did the same for them.

We learned how to share little things, how to respect other people's needs. I learned how to keep our simple bathroom and kitchen clean after using them. We invited each other to our most important family events, like birthday parties, weddings, or anniversaries. We also shared the most tragic moments, like my dad's death in 1975. Sometimes we just sat in the kitchen and talked. Thanks to my mom, I learned how to live in communalka. Was it love? Yes, it was a kind of love.

The Professor and I sat outside our tent on Solovetsky Island, a short walk from the White Sea. I could hear the water washing the beach. The Professor contemplated my story, and it made me feel good that he might consider my words important.

"It scares me a little," he said, "that you might live more for other people than a family."

"I don't know this fear about myself. I thought it was a good thing to put other people into your thoughts and to work for them when they needed your hands." I leaned into this man, wondering how such intelligence could be combined with such need. I told him that I cared for him, and we slipped into the shadow of the tent and each other.

A few weeks after we returned from Solovetsky, the Professor visited my apartment, our communalka. It was September 7. I took him to my room, where we sat on the couch and made small talk. Then, he took my hand and like a charming prince, raised it between us. His eyes flashed like lightening.

"I have had a very good time with you. You do things fast and good, like the way you put up the tent on our camping trip. You are warm and simple and I feel comfortable with you. I would like to be open with you in all things. Would you agree to marry me?"

What a surprise! I thought our relationship needed more time. I thought I needed more time to understand him and my feelings for him. I thought he needed much more time to make sure he really wanted me. Although he clearly liked me, our differences could be large. He belonged to the educational elite, and I was a normal, college-educated working girl. Even then, I knew any differences would matter more to him than to me. But you know, my heart pushed away my mind. I liked the way he asked me. It was warm, honest, and filled with emotion.

After thinking for only a minute, I said, "Yes, I agree." As the sensation of this most serious type of communalka raced through my brain and body, the Professor asked me to call my mother into the room.

The scene I paint now is not necessarily accurate, but the feeling is. When my mom entered the room, the Professor stood up, outstretching his full height into a romantic scene from a Tolstoy novel.

He placed his hand halfway across his chest and slightly bowed. Puzzled, my mom stopped in front him. He went to his knees.

"I ask you for your daughter's hand and heart," he said. His voice glistened, and in this moment, I fell in love with him.

"If she agrees," my mom replied, looking at me on the couch, "I don't mind." She spoke in the most matter-of-fact manner, in pleasant counterpoint to the Professor's theatre. He rose up with a huge smile, and my mom fell into his arms and welcomed him as a son.

I felt such a pride for her. Those old lady matchmakers, my mom, her sister, and the Professor's mother, had succeeded where God had failed. I was twenty-seven and engaged, and when the Professor left our communalka, my mom danced.

Chapter Four

Don't Rush a Blossom

Bride. A woman with a fine prospect of happiness behind her.

—*Ambrose Bierce*

I n the Soviet Union in the 1970s, people expected bad customer service, and even then only a few clerks were willing to give it. You would agree with me if you had to wait in shopping lines, sometimes for hours, and then, looking with happy relief into a saleslady's eyes, met a cold, indifferent, or unsatisfied glance that said, "Why are you bothering me by coming to this store?"

You would also agree with me if you had to wait for years to get on the list for a new apartment and then were forced to bring presents like cognac, candy, or money in envelopes to the Department of Apartments just to move your name a little faster towards the far distant hope that your grown and already married children could someday leave and start private lives in their own apartments.

As you can imagine, I didn't like dealing with clerks, and even more, I didn't like presenting a portion of myself to them for their examination. With this attitude of reluctance, I handed a middle-aged lady at the Bureau of Marriage my application for marriage. It was Tuesday, October 30, the day before my wedding, and I had returned to change the application because I would be keeping my own last name after all. Yes, Dear Readers, I met the Professor in August, and we were marrying two short months later.

"You completed this marriage application in September. It is already properly filled out with your future husband's last name." The nosy blonde stabbed her finger at the document. "Have you thought well about not taking his last name and keeping yours?"

"Yes," I answered quietly, wanting everything to end.

"And your wedding is tomorrow, the 31st of October?"

"Yes."

"Why are you doing this? Why are you going back to your last name?" The lady could hardly hide her irritation. Actually, she did not try to hide it. She thought I was a liberal woman who was refusing to honor her husband's family and rights.

It is not your business, I thought, but I answered, "I just want to keep my maiden name." I refused to argue, but she refused to stop.

"And what about your future children? Don't you want to have the same name as them? Maybe you should rethink if you want to get married at all."

Her voice was low and heavy, and my heart sank into a cold and dark place. I stopped answering, and finally she pushed the application towards me, with my maiden name and the approving stamp from the Bureau of Marriage on it. I swallowed angry tears and left.

Why did I keep my own name? The Professor told me to do it, but I cannot explain why I listened to him. Two days before the wedding, out of nowhere, he asked if I had kept my maiden name on the application.

How could he forget? On September 8, when we had filled out our application, he'd given me a huge bouquet of red roses and told me, "Congratulations, Mrs. Professor!"

When I reminded him of that happy moment, his only answer was, "Now, I think you should keep your last name."

"Why?" I asked.

"Because it is nice," he said, giving me his sign that no more was to be said.

How could he let me go to the Bureau of Marriage to change my name, as though he did not know how those clerks would treat me? The humiliation was too much to bear. Those people thought they knew how everyone should live, and the state gave them the right to teach or even dictate what others should do with their personal lives.

As I walked and cried, all the colors of life changed into one. If you can, imagine that sad and gray late autumn afternoon in rainy and foggy Latvia. Then, out of the fog and rain, as I neared the Daugava River that sliced through old Riga, I saw Vladimir walking towards me.

Vladimir was more than an old friend from college; he was one of my favorite Argonauts from Turkmenia. Perhaps you remember that the Argonauts were Greek heroes who sailed with Jason in search of the Golden Fleece and were named after their ship, the Argo?

Vladimir was an actor by nature. He had a romantic personality and dashing good looks straight out of Dr. Zhivago. Even if he didn't love you, he could make you feel that he did. I know that he reserved his best affection for me. In turn, he could make me purr like a kitten. Ladies, if like me you are not a classic beauty, and this bothers you no matter how often you tell yourself it doesn't matter, you must find a Vladimir. He is better than a day at the spa.

I found my sparkle with the Argonauts when I was nineteen. Do you know this inner smile? Do you remember when you found it? Or lost it? For me, it started to come out on a summer day in 1971 when, after a five-day train ride from Latvia, I landed in Turkmenia.

Turkmenia, once a brother in the big family of the Soviet Union and now the nation of Turkmenistan, is a poor, dry land filled with deserts and heat. In the summer, the temperature typically reaches one hundred degrees in the shade, and there isn't any shade. Back in the 1970s, Turkmenia was an ancient tribal culture with thin Russian wallpaper. I still remember watching fathers sell their young daughters into marriage on Sunday afternoons in the dusty marketplace of Mary, the provincial town where I lived for two months.[2] Our Soviet

---

[2] In the days of the empire, the Czars exiled undesirables to Mary, where they baked in the oppressive heat for the rest of their lives.

government sponsored a helping hands program that sent groups of students from affluent regions to less developed lands where they built various facilities.

More than 250 students from the Latvian Technical University were chosen to journey to Turkmenia to build a high school, a carpet factory, and public baths. There were more applicants than spots. While some people, like my brother, were cynical about the idea of using idealistic students as cheap labor, I was thrilled by the opportunity to make a great adventure.

This summer became an inner journey into my personality. Before Turkmenia, I'd had various self-doubts. I wasn't unhappy, but I didn't have all the confidence I desired. Yes, I had a lot of friends in school, but there was nothing for me, no fun life, outside of school. Too many nights, I went home to communalka, but Turkmenia changed all that.

It started with the long train ride, when our leaders organized us into twenty-five-person teams of boys and girls. Our team called itself the Argonauts. For the rest of the summer, we Argonauts worked and lived together, sleeping side by side in jeans and t-shirts without any talk or issue of sex. I know in today's sex-based culture this sounds almost stupidly innocent, but we Argonauts were that innocent. We elected our own leaders and even composed songs about our experiences. Accompanied by folk guitars, we sang enthusiastically around campfires after we dug up bottles of vodka hidden in the sand.

As for Vladimir, he was our best guitar player, our best singer, and by far the cutest Argonaut. He was skinny, tall, tanned, and blessed with thick and long black hair. His last name was Batrak, which translates into "The person who is serving on a farm." While we worked, he liked to open his shirt and shout, "I may be a Batrak, but I have a free soul!" I never had a crush on him; I just liked him so much.

On the first day in Turkmenia, things changed for me. We were boiling in the sun so we went swimming in a river the color of old coffee. Olga, a girlfriend, and I decided to swim to the other side. I made it, but the current in the middle caught her. By the time I reached her she was in a panic and going under. I pulled her to my side and carried her to the shore, where I put her on the sand and nearly collapsed. When she revived, she told me I had saved her life. The news of my small heroism made its way through the Argonauts and the camp.

Boys and girls both liked me, and I was included in everything. What a great surprise for me! Asya's Law: don't rush a blossom; it will bloom in its natural time.

Asya, Vladimir, and Mila, another Argonaut and Vladimir's future wife

I weighed only a hundred pounds, and I felt great about my body. I even enjoyed working in the hot sun. Each day we worked two shifts, from 6:00 a.m. to noon and then from 3:00 p.m. to 7:00. I was a mortar and tie bar girl. We mixed the mortar for cement and picked and arranged tie bars for the guys, who laid the foundations. At first we wore bathing suits, but the local people told us we were crazy. We quickly learned to cover up and drink green tea to preserve our moisture. It was such a fun time, singing and joking with the guys. They used to say, "Girls, we have found local buyers for you and we will be selling you in the Sunday market." They worked much harder than we did, and in turn, we girls fished the meat out of our horrible cabbage soup (camp food is bad the world over) and gave it to the boys.

My shining moment came at the end of the adventure. Each team had to write and perform a skit in front of all the students. Thanks to a little drama training at the university, I became the leader of our skit team. I organized my team to create a fifteen-minute comic routine about camp life, complete with songs and funny scenes, and I put the spotlight on Vladimir.

He performed a little sketch, playing the role of a student who has fallen out of favor with his professor. In Soviet schools, pictures of every student hung in front of the class. In response to discovering that the professor had removed his picture from the front of the room as a punishment, Vladimir did a comic turn, fell to his knees, and protested, "But you can't hang everybody! You can't hang us all!" Then he brought thunderous applause with a song about the long suffering of poor students. A prize went to the best team, and the Argonauts won it. Everyone clapped me on the back and hugged me for my efforts. It was one of the best nights of my life.

"How is the bride-to-be?" Vladimir now asked with a smile and a hug. "Wait, Asya. You look like you are already dead. Isn't that supposed to happen after you are married?" When he saw that I did not laugh at his little joke, he said, "What's wrong, my dear?"

"I love walking in this rain so that no one can see I am crying."

"What? Don't give me that junk!"

"Okay." I told him what I had done at the Bureau of Marriage. As an Argonaut, I could trust him with all things.

Vladimir answered, "Of course, it is none of my business, but I would forget about him if he could ask you to do such a thing for him. What kind of man would not want his woman to take his last name? In the West, over there, women might do that, but our men would never ask such a thing."

"My future husband is unusual. I have to take my risk," I replied. "Let's see what happens." I shrugged my shoulders as if to say, "What will be will be." I continued, "Vladimir, you are coming to the wedding party tomorrow? It's at my apartment, you know."

"A wedding party on a Wednesday night? How could anyone miss this once-in-a-lifetime opportunity? Darling, I must run." He moved away into the mist and said over his shoulder, "Think about what I have told you."

Chapter Five

Stay There Forever If You Want

All weddings, except those with shotguns in evidence, are wonderful.

—Liz Smith

In America, I have heard that young people borrow thousands of dollars to make a memory that will last forever. The Professor and I walked away from our special day not one ruble in debt, and you know what? I remember the smallest detail, even the smell of the cleaning water as my mom and I washed down our kitchen floor after the dinner. It was pine.

After I arrived in this fair country, I found work at a construction company as an office assistant. I did a little bookkeeping, purchasing, invoicing, payroll, etc. Sometimes, when things went wrong, I heard people grumble, "It's Murphy's Law at work."

"What is this Murphy's Law?" I asked an American friend. "I have heard it said many times."

"If anything can go wrong, it will," she replied.

"That is Asya's Law," I laughed.

You remember that my wedding was on October 31? It is only since I have come to America that I have learned to blame devils and witches for my upsets, for we don't celebrate Halloween in Latvia. Nonetheless, my memories of this day have a happy start.

Overnight, I had rubbed away my bad feelings about not changing my last name. I loved the sound of Raines and it kept my dad, who had died in 1975 when I was about twenty-three, close to my heart. I decided that the Professor had been spoiled as a child, and only as a caprice had sent me back for the name change. I worked any worries about my future as the Professor's wife into a simple formula: if he made me unhappy, I would just walk away.

Walk away? Once more, I thought as a girl gone crazy. The Professor was moving into communalka with my mom, my brother who still wasn't married, my neighbors, and me. Even so, I actually believed in the possibility of a lighthearted escape.

The Professor arrived at our apartment at 12:30. My smile came when I saw him. He wore a powder blue suit. What elegance and style he displayed to me! What was he thinking? Was I pretty enough? Did he still want me? He spoke formally, as if he were giving a grade. He asked about our health and nerves and plans for the day.

Asya, on the day of her wedding to the Professor

My mom was helping me get dressed. In her hands, I could feel her pride and pleasure as she straightened my gown. It followed my mom's taste and she had made it for me, but we'd created the fashion together. Fabricated from heavy, cream-colored silk, it had long sleeves with two folds, with a pleated skirt, and was not very long, just over the ankles, which made it very piquant. It wasn't a princess dress. I could see my feet and, what was most important, other people could see my feet in the most elegant white shoes I'd ever had in my life before or after.

"You look very well in this dress," remarked the Professor, with such a correct, gentle tone.

"Thank you," I said. My nerves were high. I felt like I was the oldest girl in Latvia to get married, and I wanted everything to go perfectly.

"Is your witness ready?" I asked the Professor. He was checking his hair in the mirror. In our country, we did not have this concept of best man or maid of honor. Instead, as a witness to the ceremony, we brought a good friend to the Bureau of Marriage. I had been a witness so many times that my friends joked I could make a career of it.

Ludmila was my witness, and I couldn't wait to see my best friend. She had seen the big and small events of my life, and on this important day, I needed her warm humor and practical help. Luda was a little older than I was, already married for five years, and had a three-year-old son. She was my first authority and advisor in love relationships.

"Witness?" replied the Professor, briefly glancing away from his absorption in himself. "Yes, I asked Leon today after my class."

"You asked him today for the first time?" Leon was a fellow professor at the university.

"Yes. Why not? He was a little surprised, but so? Why should we follow this convention of obsessive preparation? You know that I don't like to be like everyone else!" Now he looked at me. Taking in my worry, he added a comforting, "Asya, he will try to be on time."

I was trying to imagine how great Leon's surprise must be. He had not even known the Professor was getting married. He'd come to work on Wednesday morning and in the afternoon had agreed to be a witness at the Professor's wedding. Later, during the party, Leon kept saying, "I can't believe I am at a wedding!"

The thought of his amazement and the random absurdity of it all makes me laugh to this day.

"Okay. You found a man to stand next to you. This is good," I said. I was determined to stay happy, but I decided to bother him with another worry. "Are your parents ready to pick up my mom? You know we have to be early to the bureau."

"Oh, yes. They will be here soon after we leave," replied the Professor.

"Asenka, everything will be fine," said my mom, caressing my shoulder.

The Professor and I went to the Bureau of Marriage. We met our friends and family, and at 1:55 p.m., the doors to the marriage hall opened and a voice called, "The Professor's party."

Yes, the bureau was a government office, and it was our turn to be married by a district official of Riga. We weren't encouraged to marry in religious buildings, and even if we had been, I don't think you would have found us in a temple. God would have tired of me quickly, since I didn't believe in this idea.

Fifteen people were present with us: my old friends, or at least those who could make it in the middle of the workday on Wednesday, the Professor's witness, who had a crooked smile, my beautiful Ludmila, and the Professor's parents. But the most important two persons did not walk into the hall with us: my brother, who was in the hospital with hepatitis, and my mom.

Where was she? My courage was draining away. What should I do? Should I ask if we could wait for my mom and postpone the ceremony, slowing down the production schedule of this marriage conveyer belt the bureau managed? Another party had arrived behind us, a newly married couple was just leaving the marriage hall, and another happy couple was coming from the photography room. Was it a betrayal to start the ceremony without my mom?

We called, and no one answered the phone. The Professor's parents, who had arrived in this mad scramble, told us, "She didn't answer her phone, and that is why we did not pick her up."

I probably could have asked the officials to wait a little while, but I hesitated to ask anything of them, especially after my experience regarding my name change. I decided to get married, and I felt myself shift as I walked into the marriage hall on the Professor's arm, shooting from the orbit of a daughter to the orbit of a wife.

The strains of Mendelssohn's "Wedding March" surrounded and thrilled us. A dignified lady stood at the head of the room, bathed in candlelight. She held a leather book with our marriage documents. Its dark color matched the wooden beams in the baroque ceiling. She read a nice speech about the importance of family, love, commitment, and faith. She asked if we took each other as man and wife, and as we spoke our vows a lady played a sweet violin solo. We exchanged rings, kissed, and then signed the book. It was all very romantic, and our friends and family hugged and kissed us in their pleasure.

Then we had to leave for the champagne and chocolate room. There, for a few minutes, we had a chance to have a drink and a sweet. After a few more smiles, hugs, and kisses, we left this room to get our photographs taken. Can you see why I called this a conveyor? As we lined up for pictures, my mom rushed in and her story became the center for a few minutes.

Everyone gathered around her. "What happened? How did you miss the ceremony?"

I learned quickly that her phone had broken so she did not get the call from the Professor's parents. Had they rung her bell? No, they had not. Why? Probably it was too complicated for them to stop by, take an elevator to the sixth floor, and ring a bell.

I didn't say anything. Why throw ice on the smiles? With her near, I could now complete each breath.

"It's all right; I took a trolleybus," she said. With a big smile of happiness for me, she joined us in the photography session. The Professor made jokes and lifted my leg for the camera. This and my mom's big spirit helped me swallow some small clicks of irritation towards his parents.

We went back to our apartment for a big celebration, though the Professor had suggested a quiet dinner with his parents and my mom. As you can see, he wanted to shrink the day—the name, the witness, and the dinner—but I'd told him, "I still have close friends who will be happy for me. I want to see them. It is not so special to you because you have been married once."

He was cutting the goose for the guests when the Argonauts, my boys and girls from Turkmenia, arrived with loud and happy words.

"Asya, you're married!"

"How could you marry so fast? You were single just last month!" they teased me.

"You lucky girl!"

"Congratulations!"

"You look great," declared Vladimir. In particular, I was happy to see him. I looked at him pleasantly to show that yesterday's trouble at the bureau had vanished. I stuck my head in the kitchen to introduce my Argonauts to the Professor, but he was mad at the goose, stabbing at it with the knife and swearing. Had the goose done something wrong? Did he have anger at me over my Argonauts? He had not yet met them. Maybe he didn't approve of their warm voices to me? What should I do? Should I bother him or not?

I should have been spared this kind of problem so soon. Brides should be allowed innocence from worrying about whether or not they can keep their friends at least for their wedding day. I became self-conscious about this little indecision, and in that moment I think my personality lost some of its Turkmenian sparkle, that confidence that protected me from my own doubts and guilt over every tiny thing. I took my Argonauts into the living room without showing them to my husband, and built the first level of a wall between the Professor and me.

We had thirty people for dinner, and our communalka filled over with eating, drinking, and laughter. My mom had cooked for three days to make the feast. The main course consisted of two beautiful, shiny, oven-roasted geese, scientifically carved by the Professor. They were surrounded by boiled potatoes and stewed sauerkraut and accompanied with sliced meats, cold fish, salads, pickled and fresh vegetables, mushrooms, fresh cranberry juice, wine, vodka, and cognac. The food was the best! I was so proud of my mom when she stood to make the grand toast. Her face shined a light into the room.

"I am the luckiest of women, this October 31, 1979. For now I have another son. He is wise, intelligent, and most handsome, as you can all see." She pointed her glass at the Professor to loud applause. "Welcome to the family, my son," she said with much warmth.

Then Vladimir stood to make a toast, and everyone turned their eyes to him. He was the dashing pirate, the hope that all the Argonauts could still find their treasure as adults. I was impatient to hear his words for us.

"We have known Asya for many years. We saw her find her smile in Turkmenia, and since then she has given it back to us, her good friends, many, many times." Cheers and blushes followed. Vladimir gave me a long look of love, and then pointed his glass at the Professor.

"We want her husband to love her for the same personality that we see and love in her. Congratulations to the happy bride and groom." This toast was greeted with much pleasure. It warmed me to my toes.

Suddenly, next to me, I heard the Professor cough to get our attention. His face screwed into something not so pleasant. Before I could stop him from making his mistake, he jumped up in a tall straight line and stabbed his glass over the table.

"Why should I love her for the same? I will love her for something different," he declared aggressively. A long silence came into the room. No one drank with him. Everyone heard his unpleasant tone, and they were embarrassed for me. Even his parents looked down at the table.

I questioned myself. What could be wrong? How could he say this thing to my best friends? Was he jealous? I felt sorry for him, confused, and a little irritated, and I gave each of these feelings a third of my care.

Soon voices came from here and there and Luda held my hand for a minute. My mom smiled her "We can endure anything" smile and the party feeling slowly returned.

We continued eating, drinking, and toasting each other for many hours. No one wanted to leave, and I engaged in small talk with all my friends.

The Professor must have been gone for a while when I decided to look for him. I found him at my desk in my bedroom, far away from the happy voices of our wedding party.

"Why are you doing this?" I asked. "Why are you not with our party?"

"I am preparing for my lecture tomorrow," he said, barely glancing up from a textbook. "I am tired and I need to be ready for the students."

I left him and returned to the party and heard my friends talking in sympathy about me. I felt embarrassed at my return. Somehow they knew my husband had left without a good reason. Everyone started to leave with sad kisses and hugs for me. You know how this goes—your friends are happy and sad for you at the same time. It's like having a baby and losing a relative in the same week. I tried hard not to focus on my disappointment. When everyone was gone, the Professor returned to the living room and spoke to me.

"You know what? I will take my mom and dad home and I will sleep at their house," he said. "I have to go to work early."

These words forced me to the end of my patience. I couldn't believe he would say such a thing to me on our wedding night. I hissed at him, "You know what? You can go there tomorrow and stay there forever if you want, but tonight stay here."

He looked down at me, a quiz in his eyes. Then he must have searched himself and seen something he did not like—the thought of losing me forever on the first night of marriage. "Okay. You are right. I will go home with them and walk back," he said softly.

At about 11:00 p.m., my mom and I started to clean up the apartment. You can imagine the mess from thirty people in a place with a kitchen shared with another family. I put the ends of my wedding dress into my belt and became an old-fashioned washing woman. I think the Professor came back about midnight and went to sleep. My mom and I kept cleaning and not talking beyond our work. We wrapped the food, emptied and washed the plates, and threw away the bottles. My mom didn't complain about the Professor and neither did I. Before the end of the night, I was on my knees scrubbing the kitchen floor. Yes, in my wedding dress. It was my heroism not to discuss what had been done to me. I proved my strength.

I went to bed at 3:00 a.m. Are you wondering about this thing you call a honeymoon? I had to be at work at 8:30 a.m. When I slipped under the covers, the Professor woke up. His body was not so worried about his morning class.

Chapter Six

The Human of the Future

A baby is God's way of saying the world should go on.

—Doris Smith

I probably should have told you that I was pregnant on my wedding day. My country attached no shame to this condition. I informed the Professor a few weeks before the wedding, and he responded with much happiness. He wanted a family and the sooner the better. I loved him for his positive attitude towards children. Thank God, this never changed.

Not long after the wedding, I learned that Luda was also pregnant. While shopping for clothes, she complained about her size. When I asked her where the pounds came from, she looked at me, put together her lips, and said, "From the same reason as you."

"Oh, really." My understanding came slowly, but in a moment I got it. I was delighted that my best friend would be sharing this experience with me.

Our friendship has been long. Luda and I met on September 1, 1969, a date we still celebrate as our anniversary. We were standing in line at the student center, waiting for entry medical examinations for the university. When we began talking, we realized we shared the same classes. The next week, like all first-year college students in the country, we were sent in a group of twenty-five girls to a collective farm to harvest flax. We worked all day in the fields and each night fell asleep in exhaustion on a schoolroom floor. But we were young, and couldn't help having fun away from home.

The best part of the experience, other than my joy at being outdoors, was building my friendship with Luda. I can't explain why we became so close, but in a very short time, we easily finished each other's sentences. Maybe it helped that, like me, she lived in communalka.

If the art of making and keeping friends became an Olympic event, Luda would win the gold medal. She cannot say hello without warm words. She cannot meet me without a hug and a smile. She can wait a year for me to explain a bad feeling. She can trust me with the deepest secret of her life, yet warmly keep a chapter from my eyes.

Best friends say things that change your life. During the first year of our friendship, we were walking along the beach next to the Baltic Sea. We loved the sea. Whenever one of us felt bad, the other would say, "You know what, I feel bad. Let's go to the sea."

"We have spent many hours together," said Luda as we held each other's hands. "It has been so much fun with you. We never fight. If I was with one of my other friends, I would have had at least four fights."

"Really? Do you mean it?"

She nodded her head with energy.

"Thank you so much," I replied.

"Asya," she said. "You are the human of the future."

You can imagine how much I liked being called this by Luda. She saw deep into my personality, embraced my individuality, and appreciated me for who I was. When I looked at Luda, I knew I had a friend who would never ask me to change for her. What a relief! Her words settled into me as we stepped across the shore waters, and they have given confidence to my ears ever since.

By the way, I have never understood this American concept that couples who fight together stay together. I hate fighting. Whenever Luda and I had a little misunderstanding, we would walk to our favorite coffee shop and share a piece of cake or pastry.

Everyone loves Luda's beauty. Her heritage is Armenian, and her father, a retired military officer, moved his family to Riga when

Luda was a young girl. The party rewarded officers for their service by allowing them to live in the city of their choice. You can find a glimpse of Luda's features in the Byzantine representations of the Virgin Mary. She has the long narrow nose of the mother of Christ and that subtle and satisfied smile of thin lips. I remember my dad, a professor at our college, saying about her, "She is the most beautiful woman I have ever seen."

Asya and Luda, 1972

My dad was not afraid of hurting my feelings with his praise for Luda. Her beauty was so outstanding that her friends and family celebrated it the same way that a team celebrates the talents of its greatest star. Asya's Law: celebrate the beauty of your friends.

During our college years, we took the same academic program in economic engineering and studied together. After graduation, we both went to work for TransInform. We spent so much time at each other's homes that they became our second homes.

My pregnancy was hard on me, and Luda's friendship helped greatly. I felt half sick most of the time. Smells irritated me, and my curly hair turned straight. Women know how frustrating it is when their hair won't listen to them.

Here is how my baby came. My birthday fell near the end of my pregnancy, and the Professor and my friends were listening on the record player to a comedian of political satire. I laughed so deeply and so strongly that my body shook. I simply could not stop laughing. The Professor looked at me with a test in his eyes and said, "This laughing is not healthy for you, is it?" For years afterward, he blamed my laughter for our baby's early arrival, but I blamed it on a chain of circumstances that became altogether unfortunate.

Two days after my birthday celebration, the Professor's mother called me and said that she wanted me to go with her to pick up a late wedding present from her daughter at the post office. I told her I didn't want to go, that I was very tired, that we should wait for the Professor, but she wouldn't let go of her excitement.

At the post office, we opened the package and found a fur coat, a nice gift for me. In addition, my mother-in-law brought me some cookies—four pounds of cookies! In respect for her, I carried the coat and the cookies. In a little while we separated and I kept walking by myself. As I am sure you know, it was nearly impossible to get a taxi in the middle of the day in Soviet times. Carrying these heavy packages, I became hot in the late winter sunshine and stopped at a cafeteria for a juice. I felt dizzy. I asked the people in line if I could go to the front because in our country pregnant ladies were supposed to get a break, but there was no break that afternoon. "Get in the back of the line," those ugly faces said. "We have waited our turn."

I broke into tears and fled into the street. Suddenly, my water broke and started running down my legs. What should I do? I had no experience. I hurried home and lost more water. I called the doctor, and soon I was in the hospital a month early.

Not long after I arrived, I learned that Luda had also gone to the hospital to have her baby, two weeks early. We couldn't even make these births separate! Yes, you guessed it—we had our babies on the same day. When she called me on the phone from her bed, she said, "Stop repeating on me!"

How can I describe my baby? Nothing would ever matter again but her life. I knew it the first time I saw her. I loved her immediately. She was perfect and small. She weighed 2 kilos and 390 grams (5 pounds and 2 ounces). The first month, the doctor made me weigh her every day. She had the fingers and toes of a doll. Because she was so premature, we stayed in the hospital for almost two weeks. As for Luda, her baby required a surgery, and they had to stay in intensive care.

In Latvia, we did not rush to name our babies in the hospital. We took them home and tried to see what name they would fit into. The Professor's mother wanted to name our baby Sophia. I joked to him, "There will be no Sophia in my house." I had met some Sophias who were called "Sofa." I didn't like this version of the name. Some Russian people called their couches sofas, and I refused to turn my daughter into furniture.

During this time, the Professor and I were discussing a daring book entitled *Master and Margarita* that had just been published in the monthly magazine *Moskva*. Written in early Soviet times by Michal Bulgakov, it was a political satire on the evils of the Soviet system. Bulgakov would certainly have been executed if the book had been published in his own time.

Groups all over the country held readings of this book in their homes, and when people met each other, they quoted favorite passages. We ached in our hearts for someone to tell the truth about the dark side of the Soviet system, and our circles put as much energy into these discussions as my American friends do into their discussions of the Super Bowl.

One of our favorite scenes in *Master and Margarita* occurred when a character named Anna kicked an oil bottle on the street, not on purpose, but in typical Russian style. A passerby fell in the oil in front of a train, which of course killed this unfortunate person. One day I was changing my baby when she kicked the oil bottle onto the floor.

"That's it!" I said to the Professor. "She kicked the oil. I have found my Anna."

"Okay. Great," he replied. That same day, Luda's husband called me and asked if we had decided on a name for our baby.

"Anna," I said happily.

"Anna?" he exclaimed. "Just today we named our baby Anna."

Chapter Seven

He Was Just Wiping His Nose

Husbands are awkward things to deal with;
even putting them in hot water will not make them tender.

—*Mary Buckley*

I covered for the Professor the first time he stayed out all night. We still lived with my mom, and Anna still slept in a crib. The Professor had a circle of friends that he hadn't invited to our wedding. They were different than my buddies. Was he embarrassed by me? I don't know. His friends were members of the Latvian intelligentsia—authors, artists, and educators. I was only a systems analyst with a degree in economic engineering and not qualified for his circle.

But there was a harder lesson to swallow. After the wedding, the Professor decided he didn't like my Argonauts. Thank God he did like Luda, who was not an Argonaut. He also decided the Argonauts were a lower class of people, and he told me not to spend time with them anymore.

I didn't argue with him. I had little time for people, not even so much for Luda anymore, even though I did not work my first year with Anna. All Soviet mothers received the first year off with pay to raise their babies, and caring for Anna, keeping communalka with my mom, and buying and cooking food filled my days.

The Soviet system made buying groceries very difficult. Paint the following picture and you will understand the challenge we faced daily: buying food like meat, bread, or cheese was like going to the secretary of state's office at noon on a Monday to register your car. Take a number and sit.

The first time the Professor stayed out all night, he called me around ten o'clock and told me he was with his artist friend Igor. They were having a great time at a party, and because he didn't want to take the trolley bus home so late, he would stay at Igor's.

"Okay. I am tired anyway," I said.

Then, later I got another call. What a surprise for me! It was Igor, looking for the Professor.

"He is not here," I said. "It is so funny. He called me earlier and said he was with you. Is your apartment so big that you have not seen him? He is very tall."

The next morning was Saturday. The Professor's father called early and asked for his son. His parents were conservative and would not be happy to learn of their son's nighttime disappearance.

"He is out getting bread and milk," I said, telling a lie. His father didn't speak for some moments. It was hard for him to think of his son buying food. Women had always done this for him, as was common practice in the Soviet Union.

"Is he coming for dinner with us or not?"

"He will be home soon. I will have him call you."

Later, when the Professor arrived home, I told him about his father's call.

"My father called for me?"

"Yes. I told him that you were out for food."

A look of understanding came into the Professor's eyes. "You are a very good person," he said. "I apologize for my actions."

"Okay. But I feel stupid lying for you. Why should I have to do it?" I asked. He didn't respond, so I went after him a little. "You also need to know that Igor called for you after you called me and asked to speak to you. This is strange, isn't it?"

"Yes." His tone said, "Don't ask me any more questions."

I was angry at him, so I left the room. Maybe you think I went to my mom's room to complain about the Professor, but I didn't. There was already unhappiness between her and her new son, and I didn't want to make it worse.

The Professor and I wanted our own apartment, and trying to arrange this had inadvertently caused the friction between him and my mom. The trouble was, the only way to get our own apartment was to move our name up the list maintained by the Soviet officer. How would we do this? I would have to change my registration from my mom's communalka to the apartment the Professor's parents lived in. It was not as big as my mom's, and since the government gave priority to reducing crowded family conditions, changing my registration in this way might increase the justification for our young family's need for our own apartment.

My mom was worried about this move. It might not work. I might get lost in the system and not only lose my rights to her communalka, but also relinquish my future rights to move in with the Professor's parents. In this way the Soviet officers in charge of living spaces ruled our lives.

"Can you guarantee success?" my mom had asked the Professor after he told her of his plan to have me change my address.

"I am not a Communist Party secretary. I cannot give you any guarantees," he'd replied with sarcasm dripping from his voice.

His tone shocked my mom. I could tell by the twist on her face.

"Okay," she had answered quietly and left the room.

"Why are you doing that? Why are you speaking to my mom in such a tone?" I demanded.

He didn't answer me.

"You are nervous, and when you get nervous, you act aggressively. Isn't that so?" I said.

He shrugged his shoulders as if saying I were right. It made me crazy that he had a doctorate in psychology yet was so ignorant of the most common politeness. I went to my mom and apologized for him.

"I didn't mean not to trust him," she told me. "I was only worried about what could go wrong for you."

I am not sure if the Professor ever apologized, but their relationship chilled and never warmed. He made no secret of his attitude towards the Communist Party and my mom's association with it. He thought the party was filled with stupid people who had built an inefficient and inhumane system of government. My mom's sacrifices in the war, her award for her heroism, her position as a professor and as a party historian, did not move him as excuses for devotion to the party. He expected her, as a woman of intelligence and accomplishment, to approach the party with brutal, analytical honesty.

Of course, the Professor expressed this antagonism towards our Soviet system in private. He had learned this lesson the hard way. When General Secretary Leonid Brezhnev died, the Professor gave a lecture in which two students in the back of the room consistently talked. He asked them to stop talking or to leave.

"We are discussing the General Secretary's death," one of the girls said.

"This is not a valid excuse," replied the Professor.

One of the students complained to the dean's office about the Professor's comment, and the dean invited the Professor to his office and warned him to watch his tongue.

"She should admit that the party has failed to develop our country. It has become a joke that we all endure," the Professor told me once in criticism of my mom. "How can she follow them? Several years after the war ended she couldn't even find work because she is Jewish! What kind of system is this? She wanted to give her life for those idiots, and they rewarded her by keeping her out of a job."

Unfortunately, he spoke correctly. After World War II, my mom was not a desirable employee because she was Jewish. Stalin had launched a persecution campaign against Jews, using as an excuse his claim that his Jewish doctors were poisoning him. The party persecuted even war heroes like my mom. Lucky for her, the chief partisan commander in her region heard of her situation and got her the only job available, teaching the history of the Communist Party at the university. It is not difficult to imagine why most educated persons avoided this kind of assignment, as it was filled with non-scientific nonsense and party propaganda.

"His criticism is fair enough," my mom essentially said, "but I can't poison the well I have been drinking from my whole life."

"Please be patient with her," I said to the Professor. "Her life has been hard. She doesn't want this pressure from you to turn her back on everything she has believed in."

In spite of my pleas, there was hardness in the Professor towards my mom, and it gave me great sadness to have this divide in our communalka. This was why I hoped with all my heart that our name would move up the apartment list so we could live by ourselves.

Frankly, I also hoped that moving would relax my husband's nighttime adventures. Yes, they had continued after the first experience of Igor's call. I wondered if my cover-up increased his confidence to spend nights in other beds. Perhaps he thought I approved of his wanderings. But I kept quiet, because I wanted him to be the man of our family.

Most European wives know and for the most part endure the fact that their husbands will find a mistress. In America, having a mistress is a sin; in Europe, it is considered almost a necessity among men. So here was my next law: learn to live with it. I mostly did, but sometimes I lost control.

One morning the Professor came home when everyone but me was sleeping. I felt lonely and sad. "What are you doing this for?" I asked as I lay in our bed.

"We have a good time and conversation with Igor in his studio, then he leaves and Irena and I sleep together."

"Why do you need this?"

"She is important to me in Moscow. You know that she is a person of authority at the Institute and has a say in conferences, publishing, and so on. She likes me to please her. This makes it easier for my work, and it is fun to be with her."

"She knows you have a daughter and wife."

He shrugged his shoulders. It did not matter to either of them.

"Why do you need this other thing? Am I not enough for you?"

"Darling, it is like this. When you have a running nose and it is cold, you blow it. But when you come inside the warm place of family, the running nose goes away. Do not take this nose blowing seriously. You are a very good wife and mother, and this is my real home. Do you understand what I say here?"

His logic crushed me. How could I argue with him? Somehow, he had turned his cheating into a compliment. Yes, I think we had sex that night. I know that we did most times when he came home very late at night or early in the mornings. I wanted to be wanted, and I wondered if he wanted me because she had failed to satisfy him. But, I also wondered if I were naïve. Did I lack the sophistication and intelligence to deal with real freedom in a relationship? I did not have the education of my husband. Did he know a better way to live?

Looking back, I am so sad that I did not talk to my mom about this. Our bedrooms in the communalka were private enough that she didn't know about his other life. She could have helped me understand this little monster that climbed on my back, but more than this, she would have wanted to help. Though she was unaware of the Professor's mistress, she knew all was not well with the Professor and me, and sometimes I cannot stand the thought of her watching me suffer and keeping her sadness to herself because she did not want to make it worse.

After I came to America, a woman at work told me that her husband had been unfaithful.

"What does this 'unfaithful' mean?" I asked, not knowing this English term.

She told me the meaning—that her husband had been with another woman.

"He was just wiping his nose," I replied.

Chapter Eight

Love Is One Hundred Daily Favors

It is a wise father that knows his own child.

— William Shakespeare

Our most happy year came after Simon was born. He arrived in July of 1984 when Anna was four. That summer we lived in a dacha in Jurmala, only a short walk from the Baltic Sea. Jurmala, a charming seaside town east of Riga, offered lazy summer living for the working and professional classes during Soviet times, though today it has been transformed into a pricey haven for wealthy Baltic and European capitalists.

The Professor commuted to Riga, and I spent easy days on the beach with Anna in the weeks leading up to Simon's birth. Don't get a fantasy about our dacha. It was one room in a large old house filled with other young families. We didn't have a phone, and everything except the bedroom was communalka.

Like all expectant mothers, I had stopped working two months before my baby's due date. Now, this question I must ask: how do you American mothers have a baby and stay okay? You sit at your desk until your water breaks, you walk out of the hospital when you have no breath, and in too short a time, you pull back your breasts from your baby's hungry lips and return to work in crazy tears.

In Soviet Latvia, I not only received paid time off before my babies arrived, I got at least five days in the hospital (enough time to really catch my breath, yes?), then one year at home with my baby, the first two months at full pay, the next ten months at quarter pay. In my baby's second year, I could return to work part time with no losses of benefits or position. What do you think? Was our Communist system so bad?

I was packing our room for the return to our Riga apartment when my contractions started. Quickly, they became heavy. It was late at night, so the Professor ran to the pay phone at the rail station to call the hospital.

"What did they say?" I asked him when he returned.

"They asked, 'What child is it?' I told them the second. Then they said, 'So you don't know what to do? Get her to the hospital!'"

It took too many minutes for the taxi to arrive to take me to Riga. When we got to the hospital, the nurses looked at me and said, "We will take you now. Get ready to push hard."

The Professor wanted to come in with me, but for Anna's sake, I sent him back to Jurmala. We had left her asleep in communalka. The neighbors would care for her, so I could have let the Professor come, but I wanted to have my baby alone.

Modern women, I know you like it when your men help bring these babies into the air, but I did not want my man looking at my face, let alone my body, in this process. Do some of you mothers know this feeling?

We did not know if the baby would be a boy or girl. The next morning, I called the dacha to tell the Professor we had a beautiful boy. He had wanted a son so bad, and I wanted one for him.

"Da. Da. Daaaaaaaaaaaaaaaaaaaaaaaa!"[3] He shouted for joy, and my heart puffed up in pride.

Yes, I must admit, I felt like I had done something. The neighbors in and near the dacha told me later they had never seen such happiness in a father. He jumped and ran and shouted to the neighbors, to

---

[3] "Da" means "yes" in Russian.

the streets, to the sea, "I have a son! I have a son! I have a son!" Then
he bought cognac for everyone in Jurmala.

After we got home with Simon, everything worked to the good.
The family man came out of the Professor. He helped me with shopping, cleaning, and caring for Anna. He changed diapers and rocked
Simon back to sleep when he cried. By now, we had our own apartment. It was two rooms and all ours. The Professor's idea of putting
me as a resident in his parent's apartment had worked as planned, and
it had only taken a year and a half for them to move to top of the list. (I
later learned this occurred because his parents had a paper from the
wartime that showed them as early supporters of the party.) When
they got permission to move, we moved out of my mom's communalka
into this new apartment, and they stayed put in their old one.

The Professor and I worked as a team, fixing up the place in our
style and giving it the personality of our young family. Finally, I was
free of communalka and its rules! I so remember happy times of
cooking and eating meals together. And you know what? The
Professor stopped wiping his nose in strange beds. He even surprised me by going 900 miles by train to Moscow and buying me an
apartment-sized combination washing and drying machine and
bringing it back to Riga. No more washing all of our clothes by
hand—what a relief! But can you imagine living in Detroit and traveling to Miami to buy a washing machine? This was our Soviet life.

Becoming a *mamochka* for our beautiful boy gave me more power
with the Professor. Here's a short story to illustrate this. The day I
left the hospital with Simon, the nurses took me to the outside door
of the birth department where I waited for the Professor, who was
supposed to come with a cab. Simon screamed for his food, and the
dress the nurses had given me was too tight. I sweated and felt faint,
and I tried to take it easy because I didn't want to lose my milk. New
mothers know this spinning feeling. The Professor finally came, very
late and without a cab.

"Where is the cab?" I demanded.

"I will just catch one here." He waved at the empty street.

"Have you absolutely lost your mind? There are no cabs near this place. Look at our baby. Do you notice this screaming? As I told you first, bring a cab to this door."

A little embarrassed at his lateness and his failure, the Professor turned back into the Riga streets. Yes, I showed my irritation that day, but as in most cases, my irritation did nothing to help my problem. Simon screamed for another thirty minutes before the Professor returned.

In this mostly happy time, I knew only one sad feeling. Many times when I looked at Simon, I saw my dad. His wide easy smile and his open face were in Simon. I missed my dad so much! In our family, he was the one who had made the ideas. He had even dreamed of playing tennis. Yes, this man with red hair and freckles who had fought the Nazis and had been wounded and returned to the front for more combat, who had been nominated with only a bachelor's degree to the professor's chair in the economy of the chemical industry department, who with his own hand had written the textbook and was the local Communist Party boss, had wanted to learn how to play this most petite bourgeois game, this favorite pastime of the Latvian elite.

My dad only got mad at me once. Was I such a good girl that it only happened once, or was he such a good father that he only had to do it once? It was the time of his fiftieth birthday. I went to his celebration at the university and then to another celebration with his friends. The final party was with the aunts, uncles, and cousins at home. On this occasion, I decided to go out with my friends.

At about 11:00 o'clock, a friend asked me if I was going to my dad's party. I told her it was no big deal and that I had already been to two parties, but when I opened the door to our apartment near midnight, my mistake mushroomed in front of my eyes. If two visitors had remained it would have been okay, but there was no one to save me. The apartment was deadly quiet. Hearing my entry, my dad walked into the hallway and looked at me as if I had killed someone.

"What did you think? That everyone would wait for you?"

"No."

"How do you think I feel? Everyone asked, 'Where is she?'"

"But Dad, I went to the party with your colleagues."

"You don't know yet that family is most important to me?"

Of course I apologized, but how I wished I could turn back the clock and be with him that night, especially since he lived only two years after his fiftieth birthday. He died at home, much too soon, and he never got to play tennis.

I remember the night he died in 1975 as if it were yesterday. He came home tired from his work at the university. He told me he had gone to the dentist and still had pain in his tooth. He went to bed early. A light through the glass window on top of my door woke me up in the middle of the night. Then I heard noises. I checked in the hall and saw Jan, my brother.

"Something is wrong with Dad," he said. What a look of worry I saw on his face. I followed him into my parent's room and saw my dad on the bed. He was conscious.

"My heart hurts so hard," he sputtered. His older brother had died of a heart attack, and my dad had lived in this shadow. Then my dad started shouting, twisting with the pain, and clutching his heart. My brother told me he had called for emergency help.

"I never knew it would hurt so hard," my dad gasped.

The helpers arrived. I saw their ambulance on the street. Oh no! Our elevator was broken. The ambulance men had to climb six floors with a stretcher. I ran to the stairs, located in the open middle of our building. I stood next to the railing and looked down at the two men slowly walking up.

"Men, come fast, come faster!" I yelled. My dad's shouts came through the walls. "Please! My dad needs you so bad!" I counted the steps. Had there ever been a slower climb? "Hurry up. Can you, please?" Halfway up, one of the guys, a skinny man, looked at me with the pinched face of a thousand midnight stair climbs and said, "If I could I would."

When finally the men arrived, they gave my dad a shot of some medicine and tried a chest massage. He shouted even louder. Some monster had grabbed his heart. My mom, my brother, and I stood apart from the two men struggling with him. My mom was in shock.

Tears pooled in her eyes, and she swallowed them silently. My dear brother wanted to save him so much. He pleaded with the men to do some good. My dad's screaming chewed on our souls. I will never forget the sounds.

"Go to the kitchen and boil water for needles!" said the skinny man. My brother raced to the kitchen. Some more massages and hits on the chest. The men moved in the slowest of motions.

"They don't know what they are doing," I thought. Then my dad turned a shout into a final scream and took his pain to the place of no return.

There were no Hollywood talks with great meaning, no gentle good-byes, no shiny or modern equipment to pack in medical bags, except the needles left in the water. The life-saving heroes ended their mission without saving my dad's life. They gave my brother a government form about our dead father and then trudged away with a shrug and an "I'm sorry."

Their best was not good enough, we all thought to ourselves. Now, I think my dad would surely be alive if such a thing had happened in America. We went into the bedroom to rest, leaving my dad on the couch.

You know, I have tried to teach my own children what my dad taught me about life. He taught me one of my favorite laws: that love is one hundred daily favors.

Let me say how he practiced this one. When I was in the fourth grade, I visited a friend's home after school. I forget why, but the parents became irritated at me and rudely sent me home. A block from home, my dad appeared, walking toward me. He asked me what was wrong.

"Natasha's mom kicked me out. Nobody should say, 'Go home!' like that!" Then I released my tears.

I remember his face, half-sympathetic (poor thing) and half-smile (not a big deal, actually). He took me by the hand into a store nearby and bought 100 grams (about 3.5 ounces) of chocolate, gave me the bag, and said, "Go home, dear. Everything will be fine." (And it was.)

С новым
1957 годом

Jan, Asya, and Kuse Raines

He liked to say that each little thing has something big in it. As a kid, I asked him why he fell in love with my mom and he said, "Because she had red cheeks."

He showed the strength of his personality at work. He was the assistant dean at the university. After the war, he earned his degree at night school while working in a glass factory. Over the years, he gained so much knowledge about the process of planning, manufacturing, and distributing glass that the university asked him to be a guest instructor. In a short time, he became highly regarded, and the school asked him to become a professor and create a program in the economy of chemical manufacturing. This was a genuine and unusual honor in a nation where academic credentials were only second to party titles.

My dad was also the local party boss at the university. He was given this position because everyone trusted him. He didn't spy on people or make up lies about our great economy or turn families into the KGB if they said words against the state. My mom and dad went to monthly party meetings. They paid the small monthly dues and helped organize political events. As a boss, my dad helped make decisions on promotions and discipline and appointments. All things being equal, the sweets went to the party members, but is your company so different? Would you believe that when I told my dad I would not join the party, he never said a word?

Once at the university, a party official asked me if I was ready to join the party. I told her I was not interested. She was shocked. Were not my parents party members? Did not the party give them jobs?

Of course I respected the principles for my parents, I replied, but I did not want them for myself.

When my mom asked why I didn't join the party, I told her, "I don't want to participate in something I don't believe in and that is so formal. People take too much advantage of their position."

She only made a slight smile and said, "Really?"

I learned from my dad how to stand on principle. Once a professor in his department had an affair with a student. This professor was one of my teachers. He had a wooden leg from the war and a bald head. What the girl saw in such an older man, I didn't know. He was also married. Soon he separated from his wife and moved in with the student. My university was small. Everyone knew what was happening, and everyone talked about it. All my dad's colleagues wanted to expel the professor for his immoral behavior.

"I won't let you do it," my dad told the committee. "He is an adult. The student is an adult. They are hiding nothing. Everything is open. Their love life is none of our business." The other teachers could not move my dad, and his courage saved this man's job. Yes, the professor married the student, but in the tragic tradition of Russian culture, he died soon after he claimed his happiness.

Obviously, I worshipped my dad, but I only pictured him as being strong and in control of every situation. I remember how he showed me another meaning of self-control, a lesson that helped me endure much suffering with the Professor.

Once I was in his office showing him some new shoes I had just bought when a faculty member from another department walked into the room. He ignored me as a person who didn't matter and started yelling, really yelling, at my dad about some report my dad had not completed. I stood as still as a frozen bird, waiting for my dad to get angry at this man. But my dad said no words back, although the shouting seemed to push him down into his chair. When the man stopped yelling and left, I asked my dad why he'd let the man talk to him like that.

"Because he is stupid," he growled. "You know the Russian saying: 'Don't argue with a fool.'"

By now you may be asking why I married a professor so different from the professor who fathered me. Yes, sometimes I ask myself the same question. My dad and the Professor were similar in the first impressions they made: smart, creative, and enthusiastic men with deep knowledge of their subjects. But my dad always took the high road, and even when it filled with suffering, he put the interests of others before himself. He did not allow himself to become moody, sarcastic, or forgetful of others.

The day after he died, when he was still laid out in our home, family members and co-workers came to pay their respects. I sat on our balcony smoking with one of his colleagues, who was a former professor of mine. She liked my dad. She told me, "Your dad was such a giving person. He could do kindness and the other person would never feel humiliated. Don't ever expect to meet someone like him again."

Chapter Nine

Glasnost

Sometimes when you stand face to face with someone,
you cannot see his face.

—*Mikhail S. Gorbachev*

In 1985, at the peak of the Professor's and my happiness, Mikhail S. Gorbachev, general secretary of the Communist Party, introduced *glasnost* to our country. *Glas* means voice in Russian, and *glasnost* was supposed to open our voices, long shut tight by the Soviet system, to tell the truth about our sick economy.

Do you remember the term "Iron Curtain"? We knew well this metaphor that described Soviet control of Central and Eastern Europe after World War II and the closed borders between communist East and capitalist West. This symbol actually had two meanings for us: that information from the West was blocked (this is the common understanding of the term), and that information was likewise blocked from inside our country. *Glasnost* started the falling of the Iron Curtain, and it fell harder and faster on me than I ever could have imagined.

Yes, we knew the Western economies were superior. We knew we were sinking further and further behind. We knew that Americans didn't have to wait ten years to buy a car or share their bathrooms and kitchens with other families. Contrary to what you might believe, information was available. For example, we received letters from Nina, the Professor's sister who had immigrated to America in the early 1970s. Also, we had access to magazines and newspapers. I could even buy the *New York Times* in the International Bookstore in Riga, and no, the KGB did not cut out the pictures of the fantastic lifestyle to be found in the United States. But I didn't buy such items very often. I was a working mother, and much too focused on day-to-day living to care about politics.

In college, I had studied economics because I had wanted to gain a deeper understanding of our system. I thought it would improve my chances to live successfully. Of course, our teachers compared our system to capitalism. For our projects, we read translated books from American thinkers like Frederick Taylor and Henry Ford. I remember saying to myself, "Oh, this American way makes sense. I see how it works with human nature."

I was completely confused when we switched to studying our socialist economy. How could an office in Moscow determine everything that was needed and wanted, right down to the number of toothbrushes in Riga or the quantity of vacuum cleaners in Turkmenia? I think Gorbachev must have had the same confusion. The more he tried to improve our lives, the more the system shook, until the whole thing collapsed.

In 1985, I could not clearly see the end. Ironically, as I write these stories, I recall two more things that happened in 1985 connected to the idea of *glas*, or voice: first, baby Simon got so sick in the throat that he had to stay in the hospital for a week. What a worry that was! His throat became so constricted that he had trouble breathing. I stayed in the hospital with him and didn't take my eyes off him for a minute.

Second, the Professor's nose started running again, only this time it turned into a nasty cold, and he couldn't stop himself from making a confession. Not long after I brought Simon home from the hospital, I praised him for his goodness.

"I am not such a good man," he said.

I could see a soft pain in his eyes. "Oh, you are; you are the best husband," I reassured him. "I am a happy woman. Look at how much you cared for Anna and our apartment while I stayed in the hospital with Simon."

Simon and Anna, 1986

"Something happened." He said this quietly.

"What happened, my dear?" I looked at him sympathetically.

"I have met somebody." He shook his head, and I saw his guilty shadow shaking with it.

Sadness coiled within me. His confession brought down my happiness so suddenly. Was I destined to live so backward?

"I don't know why it happened to me. I love you. I love this family way of life. She is not even as pretty as you." He smiled, trying to catch my heart, but my happiness retreated from me like a sunrise in reverse.

"Why do you need this? It sounds so serious, so much more than taking care of your nose when it is cold." I pleaded to know the answer, but he did not know it himself. We talked for about an hour, and it was clear that he couldn't imagine life without us. He made no criticism of me. He asked me to change nothing. But I saw the division in his heart, and I knew I could not tolerate it.

"This really hurts," I said. "I am putting it on you to make a decision. You have to choose between us. You can't divide yourself and make anyone happy."

What can I say about this matter? I went on with life, watching him leave in the morning, not knowing if he would return at night. In the spirit of *glasnost*, he acted as if his openness made it better for me, but it didn't, and I started to build a bitter place in my soul for him. Asya's Law: if you have a secret, don't spread it.

As for the party's *glasnost*, we greeted it with a mixture of sarcasm and nostalgia. We remembered with smiles the party's great movement in the 1960s, when it promised to transform our socialist state into a true and pure communist state by 1980. You may not believe this idea of true communism, and by now neither did we. How could we imagine a state with no money, where everyone would work at their jobs out of sweetness and intelligence and only consume exactly what they needed and not one drop more? How could we imagine a place without cynicism or personal advantage or fear? The party put up billboards in Riga that read "Today's Generation of Soviet People will live in Communism." Like sheep, we bowed to the fairy tale in public. Then, we returned to our crowded communalkas and made a million jokes about our system and ourselves.

But Gorbachev's *glasnost* was not a laughing matter. I felt it first in my company, TransInform. We made software for transportation companies such as buses, taxis, and trucks. Using Cobol and PLC languages, I designed and put into place the algorithms that transformed incoming data into payroll, taxation, and management applications. We worked off mainframe computers, and I led a team that worked with customers to identify and supply their information needs. If the manager of a Riga bus company wanted to know how many passengers rode on Bus #367 in December, we could tell him in our report. If the manager wanted to know how many people rode with the driver Valdis, we could tell him that, too.

I loved my job, and I programmed my mind to maintain an invisible glass wall between the Professor and me. I tried not to know what was happening on the dark side of my family, and my work was a happy refuge from these shadows. It helped that, in 1987, in the spirit of *perestroika*, Gorbachev created a law that allowed state enterprises like TransInform to determine their own output levels. *Perestroika* means to restructure, and this meant we no longer had to take orders from the ministry in Moscow. Instead, we could go to our customers and sell them what they wanted.

In American understanding, we no longer had to build refrigerators for the Eskimos. This process of buying and selling services based on real needs, so obvious in America but so absent in Soviet times, gave our people much energy. TransInform threw away its Communist curtains and quickly grew its business to employ 300 people.

The freedom also came for TransInform to elect its own company director (Americans would call the position "president" or "CEO"). Across the Soviet Union, in factories and offices, workers tossed away their party-appointed bosses and elected their own heads. We elected the chief programmer at TransInform, my friend and boss, to the director's office.

This result gave me happiness, but it was not without a cost. I remember meeting our old director on the street. Yes, he mostly followed orders from Moscow and he had blocked me from promotion because I am a Jew, but I still felt some sympathy for him. The election had tossed him out of his job completely, and he complained bitterly to me about this extreme end. He had spent his career at TransInform. Such bitterness compounded throughout the country as workers put their party bosses on the streets. The whole system of control started to slowly unravel, and I began to notice shortages in basics like butter, cheese, and sausage.

It was also *perestroika* that improved the Professor's relationship with his mistress. The restructuring in our country meant that private ownership of business was once again allowed. This was truly revolutionary. Since Lenin's time, no Soviet citizens had been permitted to own their own business. The Professor jumped at the opportunity, and with a small group opened a training cooperative.

We couldn't call these businesses "companies," as that would have been too capitalistic, but the Professor's cooperative trained teachers, business people, and government officials in personality improvements like listening, team building, motivation, and so on. The Professor's experience and credentials in psychology gave the cooperative an excellent advantage, and it seemed as though he found himself there. Unfortunately, as I was soon to learn, the real energy came from his boss, the female president.

One night, we were having dinner in our apartment when a loud knock sounded on the door. The Professor answered it, and soon I heard a woman's bossy voice yelling at him for being lazy, for not paying attention to the customers, for not completing his work as promised. As the children and I listened behind the door to this humiliation of the man of our family, I realized that only one person could have the right to yell so at the Professor — his lover.

I had never met her, and even that evening I did not open the door to see her face, but a physical pain moved permanently into my chest. What else can happen when you see yourself as a backup and nothing more? The Professor's boss, his queen, inspired his energy, and she ruled in the office and in the bed. After hearing her voice, visions of the Professor's body that I knew so well and of what he did to her and she did to him began to rule me and drive me crazy. The idea of sex with him now repulsed me.

"So this is your queen?" I asked him after I put the kids to bed that night. "From now on, ask her what to do." After that evening, odd happenings began to make sense. I had found gifts of scarves and ties among his clothes. When I had asked where they had come from, he had replied, "Oh, these are little nothings my boss gives to me for a good job." He also took many phone calls from her at night, and now I knew why these calls were so long and so frequent. He had even called her in the hospital to wish her a good recovery from a surgery.

"Oh, she must be a good boss for you to call her," I had said. I also knew she had two children. Why did these children sometimes call for help with their homework? It became clear that he was at their home so much that they looked to him as their teacher. Yes, she had been married when they had begun their affair.

As you have probably figured out by now, I have a tendency to stay in the background and wait for bad things to go away. It didn't work this time. One night, after living on the edge of another ordinary day of working and finding food and helping the kids with school, I took a phone call. It was Victor, a team member I liked from the training cooperative. He was an interesting, intelligent guy, and I could hear my voice become friendly. He wanted to speak to the Professor. It was late, and I remember the quiet darkness in the apartment. I had one low light on the desk so as to not wake the children.

"I don't know where he is," I replied.

"You don't?"

"No, I don't. Maybe you should call his boss," I suggested. Did he hear my little cynicism?

"Oh, I don't want to do that at night," he said. "She has three kids to take care of. Who has three kids in these times? It must be very hard on her."

"Three kids?" I said with surprise. "I thought she had two children."

"She has three for sure."

"How old is the little one?"

"Just turned three."

Dear Readers, almost five years had passed since I had told the Professor to choose between his queen and me. From time to time, certain situations reminded me that there was a queen in the background, but for the most part we lived a family life, raised our children, and struggled through *glasnost* and *perestroika*. Sometimes we laughed, and sometimes I forgot the queen even existed.

During Victor's call, I felt a heat come through my whole body. He stopped his talking. He and I both understood at the same time that the third child belonged to the Professor. He hung up the phone, then in a couple of minutes called back to say he was sorry for his openness.

Glasnost, I thought bitterly. Yet another secret had been spread.

I took the calendar and counted back thirty-six months and found the week they had conceived their child. It was right after the death of the Professor's mother. I even remembered the night he had said he wanted to be alone with his grief. Now it became clear that this woman's surgery had been the delivery of her child and that he had called her to check on her condition and that of the baby's.

When he came home, I let him have my anger. "Tonight, I learned that you and she have a child."

His face fell as my voice fingered his guilt.

"It is true, isn't it?"

"Yes."

"What are you doing to this child? This poor child you are damaging so much. Are you going to live with them?"

"No."

"My God, you are terrible. And so is she. I cannot tolerate what you are doing. You are adults. Didn't you know this would happen? Now even the smallest events are part of your stupid drama. Last week, when the oldest daughter called, she told you her sister had fallen off a swing. She asked you to help, and you told her to call her father. Your own daughter was the injured one, wasn't she? Tell me! She was hurt, and your queen was not at home. Right?"

"Yes."

"What kind of people are you? Your little daughter falls off the swing at the playground, and you tell her half-sister to call her father who, by the way, left his home because of your dirty affair. Why did this girl call you? Because you are the father. How could you do this to me, to Anna, to Simon? What kind of man are you?" I was mad, really mad, and so sorry about that baby.

"I didn't know that she was pregnant."

"Are you that stupid? What an excuse for a man to make."

"If it hurts you so much, why are you talking about it endlessly?"

"Because I heard what I heard and I saw what I saw. Tell me, what would you do if I did this to you?"

Chapter Ten

The Drama of the Century

There are no good girls gone wrong, just bad girls found out.

—Mae West

Glasnost destroyed the Soviet Union. The genie in the bottle of the USSR was always the suppressed desire to be free. In the short run, it is easier to keep prisoners behind bars than to give them freedom. Stalin knew this well, and that is why he so ruthlessly murdered, imprisoned, and deported many millions. The small freedoms of *glasnost* revived old nationalistic movements and inspired new ones. The older generation expected the authorities to firmly put down these movements, but for no apparent reason other than tiredness, nothing happened. And, the people got bolder. They ran to their demonstrations, as protesters will do, with innocent hearts.

You know what? I respected these demonstrators, but I didn't have anything to do with their actions. All this turnover bothered me. It brought dark questions into my soul. Yes, the Soviet Union was stupid and now everyone hated its system, but it had freed my mom from prison and had saved her, my dad, one uncle, three aunts, and thousands more Jews from the Nazis.

How many Jews had the Latvians saved? How many Jews had the Latvians killed? Who really knew, but I didn't like this feeling that the Latvians who had worked with the Nazis against the Soviets might become the new heroes.

In 1988, a Latvian professor published the documents of the secret agreement between Hitler and Stalin in 1939 that had given Stalin the Baltic nations. With this, the last shred of fantasy that the Latvian proletariat had invited the Soviet occupation fell into pieces. On August 23, 1989, the fiftieth anniversary of this criminal agreement, over one million Baltic peoples formed a 600-kilometer chain. I heard this human chain was three and four people deep on Brivibas Street in Riga. In America, when you talk about the fall of the "Evil Empire," your eyes see rock stars playing guitars on the Berlin Wall, but in Latvia, we see hands across the Baltic.

Understandably, my mom was feeling low. She could see the appalling drift of things to come for her Communist dreams. When I visited her apartment, she would say only, "We will have to see the next chapter of the story."

The demonstrators carried signs that read in Latvian and English, "Latvia for Latvians." It was clear that the anti-Communist fighters would be resurrected and that my mom's partisans would be shoved into history's closet. The Russians would have to fight to keep their rights, and what about the Jews? We would be given some holidays and a school, but so what? Few of us wanted to exchange our Russian language and culture for a Latvia constructed only for Latvians.

As for the Professor, I was mad at him for about a week after I learned the secret of his other child. Only a week, you say? It is in my nature, however strange it might appear to you, to care for people who should be blocked from my heart. The little girl needed a father, and I encouraged him to do his best for her. Yes, I often cried when he left to see his other family, but when he asked me for advice on what to buy for this child, I gave him what help I could. Our relationships also resumed. I never used sex as a weapon in regulating him. I didn't believe in it, and I am a bad girl at heart—I love sex.

Honestly, I was also proud of him. He saw the wrong in the coming storm against all things Russian, and he joined groups that worked against this heaviness.

As the Soviet Union continued to deteriorate, food rationing began. This made life a little harder. Each month we received a sheet of stamps for flour, butter, sugar, cigarettes, and vodka. Here is something to know about the vodka: Gorbachev implemented a strict law forbidding alcohol at work. Before his decision, people commonly drank at their workplaces. Afternoon wine and cheese birthday parties at the office; what is wrong with that? The stores were now constantly out of stuff, and it frustrated me to no end to wait in line for up to an hour, only to hear, "We have no more of that."

People who worked in these stores started to steal food, and it showed up even at TransInform. I refused to take part in this black market. "My kids will survive with milk. They do not need cream so much," I said. Really, nobody went hungry on the streets. The rationing was more of a nuisance than anything else, but I must admit it hurried the downfall of the country.

In the middle of this uncertainty about our future, the Professor's queen called and asked to meet me for coffee. This happened after we moved to a bigger apartment, with five rooms. Can you believe it? I know I couldn't. The children finally had their own bedrooms, and the Professor's father moved in with us because he'd had a stroke and needed to be taken care of. Yes, this was an additional burden on my shoulders, but I didn't mind. We all took care of our parents, as they had no other place to go. Nursing homes and assisted living centers were as rare as golf courses.

I met the queen at a nice cafeteria in a planetarium that had been a church before the Communist takeover. I didn't join my friends in plotting horoscopes, but it did seem strange that the queen and I would meet in a place where the planets circled on view. She was surprised at me.

"Hmmm. I didn't know you looked like that," she said.

I was wearing a sharp purple raincoat. In Latvia, you remembered the color of your favorite clothes, if you were lucky enough to have any.

"What do you mean?" I said, knowing exactly what she meant.

"You are a good-looking woman."

"What's so surprising about that?" I asked with just the right amount of diplomatic confidence.

"I imagined you as different."

I smiled as images emerged of how the Professor had painted me to her. "Oh, she is a normal woman with two children," he might have kindly said. Perhaps he'd added, "Once she was pretty, but she let herself fall apart as she aged." Here is what I really think he said: "My wife is average."

Average! I almost hate him for this word I am not sure he ever said. Yet, after hearing the surprise in her voice at the sight of me, I knew that was exactly what he had communicated to her. She recovered her composure quickly and continued measuring me as an animal for stuffing.

We talked, and I drank in her looks like a cup of cold coffee that had no sugar or cream. It did not taste good. The queen was taller than me, and statuesque. She had big hair, big breasts, and a big, bossy mouth. A professor of Russian theatre, she ruled him easily. Honestly, knowing him, I wondered how he could exist with her. He was used to me, the servant. Suddenly, I knew why she had called me. After all these years, he was getting tired of her, and she was making her claim of desperation before her treasure disappeared forever. As for me, I was tired of her after five minutes.

"You have my leave to respond," she seemed to say after she finished a long speech about the Professor. It was the equivalent of the closing speech at a trial in which she tried to prove that the Professor no longer loved me and had clearly chosen her and her three daughters. She told me that I was obviously an earth woman, a woman who knew her way well around the stove. For her part, her creativity brought her closer to the heavens, and that is where she found my husband.

"He reads beautiful poetry to me," she said. "Our imagination lifts us to a higher plane of existence. You see the reason for our relationship, don't you?"

The only thing I saw was a grown woman talking like a teenager, but my face did not express this thought. Yet, there was one insignificant thing she wanted to know before she ended my role as a wife.

"Do you have a husband and wife relationship with him?" she asked.

What a personal question, I thought. "Of course," I replied with a wife's smile that also said, "I know his body better than you do."

Her face turned mad, and her little tiara slipped onto the floor.

Ha! I had cut her, and I decided to push my little partisan dagger deeper. "We have two children you know. They had to come from somewhere." Sorry. The dagger found her heart.

"He is a liar. He has lied to both of us," she said angrily.

If you please, don't put us together like that, I thought.

"He is a bad man, a very bad man. I think we have to punish him," she declared dramatically.

"I'm not going to do any such thing," I calmly replied.

"Just look what he has done to us, done to our families." Her voice was low but strong.

"I'm not playing these games," I said. "I will not fight for him. If you want him, get him yourself."

Seeing her defeat, she got up silently and left the cafeteria.

As the planets shook their heads in wonder, I thought, "She may be a big shot and a beautiful so and so, but she is not a sophisticated lady. In fact, she is stupid."

I went home and acted as if nothing had happened. The Professor didn't need to hear the story of this drama from me. Then, out of the blue, when the conversation with his queen still bubbled in my blood, he asked me to go to the theater.

"Oh, how nice," I said. "We have not been in such a long time. Of course, I will want to go." I prepared myself carefully. I ironed my best black dress and put on my two lipsticks. My mind buzzed with excitement. Was he regaining his interest in me?

A short time after we were seated, I saw his queen coming down the aisle to the stage. Was she running? She seemed to be looking for someone. What? Oh, I see this next act. He said he had tickets as usual for her, had asked me to accompany him, and then left her waiting in the lobby. Near the stage, she turned around and walked up the aisle. Could she move her nose any higher? She looked at us. The Professor stared into the distance, and she became a stranger to him. Like old milk, their relationship soured.

The next day, she called me. "Did you know that I was supposed to go with him to the theater?" she asked. "I had to buy a ticket and sit by myself."

"I apologize for him. I didn't know I was in his game," I said. You might think I am crazy, but the Professor had not acted like a man. Whatever the queen was, and she was the worst woman in my opinion, his way of discarding her was not ethical. Asya's Law: a real man does not leave a lady waiting at the theater!

"I need to talk to you both. I want to come over the next night."

"Okay. Of course you are welcome."

It was a late summer night, and the children slept. The queen and the Professor sat next to each other on our couch. I sat across from them in a chair. My husband held his hands between his knees and looked down at his feet.

She was mad. The last drop in her cup of patience had flowed away. She was also in charge. I had trouble understanding the amount of aggression in this woman. She had never counted on me. She did not care about me as a wife. God only knows what little thoughts she had for my children and what she was doing by taking this boy away from his duties as a father. She started her monologue.

"Everything is over." The room got darker, as if she were drinking the sun's remaining light. "You have lied to me. You have lied to your wife. You have lied to us." I could tell by her tone that she was referring to her daughter by him. "We never want to see you again. You are not welcome in our home." She waved her hand at him. The Professor didn't argue or object. "Your daughter can never meet you once. Not in the park, not in the library, not in my home."

I was nervous, but as she talked, I almost wanted to laugh—so much drama for such a little piece of love. He didn't want her anymore, and she couldn't accept her new role in his universe. She was no longer his queen, no longer his prop. I forced myself not to smile as she stood and said, "I am leaving, and I am not staying for tea."

"Nobody asked you," I replied. The door closed and some of the darkness surged out with her. My husband still did not move.

"That's what a piece of shit I am," he said at last.

Glasnost has finally come home, I thought.

Chapter Eleven

New York, New York

> *Give my regards to Broadway,*
> *Remember me to Herald Square.*
> *Tell all the gang at Forty-Second Street*
> *That I will soon be there.*
>
> — *"Give My Regards to Broadway"*
> *George M. Cohan*

America!

It was so sudden and unbelievable. Only one day after the curtain dropped on the drama of the century, the Professor told me that his sister, Nina, who had lived in the United States since 1974, had invited me to visit her family for one month in the summer.

"Me? Why me? Why wouldn't you go first; it is your sister! You have to go," I replied, but he would not accept my objections. He wanted to please me. Yes, I knew this was a guilt management procedure, but I didn't care to pay attention to this fact because I knew some portion of his personality delighted in seeing my pleasure at the prospect of going to America.

I am a Soviet woman, born in socialism, raised in communalka, schooled in pretending in the fantasies of communist life, and shaken like a leaf by *glasnost* and *perestroika*. You will understand the following questions about America that formed in my mind: what does freedom look like? Are the people friendly and polite? Do the streets have bricks of gold or do criminals run their businesses and live in fancy houses while the workers wait in lines for bread?

The first thing I had to do was obtain a visa. The U.S. Embassy was in Moscow, and my American adventure started in the Riga Railway Station. The Professor and I were standing on the platform waiting for the evening train from Riga to Moscow when I saw Ivar, my pure-blooded Latvian from long ago, with a woman.

"Wow!"

"How are you?"

"How are you?"

"What are you doing here?"

This was a stupid question; I don't remember who asked it first. Ivar and I introduced each other to our spouses as former co-workers. We smiled with expressions that said we met on the moon, not at our former place of work. Mrs. Ivar was going to Moscow and, by chance, we were assigned to the same car.

We talked through long hours of doing nothing, and I learned what I wanted to know. She wasn't Jewish, but she wasn't Latvian either. She was half Russian and half Tatarian. What's a Tatarian? I will leave the detailed answer to your research, but here's a clue: if Latvians are white Americans, Tatarians are English-speaking Asian immigrants. What an irony to learn this, but that was their story. I will get back to mine.

I arrived in Moscow and rushed to the embassy. During my four-hour wait for admittance, a TV news reporter was filming the line, and he kept the camera on my face for some seconds. My picture made the evening news on Central TV across the Soviet Union in a story about immigration. When I returned to Riga, some of my friends teased me, "Are you still here? I thought you had immigrated to the United States!"

As you can guess, I had to return to Moscow to fly to New York, since no international plane service was allowed from Riga. On June 21, the first day of summer, I stepped on an Aeroflot plane. The feeling of vacation and adventure started in the air. I sat next to a lady journalist, an editor of a Latvian magazine. We had a wonderful time talking, enjoying a great meal, and sharing our expectations about America.

When I landed in New York, nobody was waiting for me. Nina had called before I left and told me she might be a little late, so I sat on a bench by my suitcase, watching Americans walk by and enjoying the range of colors in their clothing, suitcases, and skin. This was so different from the quiet spectrum I was familiar with at home.

The second hour I became nervous. I did not have any American dollars. In 1990, Latvians had to order dollars from the Central Bank, and it required an appointment on a specific day to get those dollars. On my day, the Central Bank had run out of American dollars. Asya's Law in force: what can go wrong, will.

The Central Bank offered me Canadian dollars or an opportunity to wait until another day when they had accumulated American dollars again. Since I did not have "another day," I'd taken Canadian dollars.

By the third hour of waiting, I wanted to make a phone call, but I did not have the right change. I asked a man for help, but he did not understand my English. I was afraid to move. What if the Professor's sister came and I was not on the bench? I wanted to go back to Riga! At the end of my wits, I was composing my hello speech to the Professor ("Your sister forgot to pick me up, so I came back") when Nina arrived.

You can imagine my happiness at seeing her warm and smiling face, and I quickly became fine. My first surprise: America is so beautiful! I thought New York was all cement, but during our drive I saw miles of woods, fields, gardens, little towns, and villages. Maybe you know the Hudson River Valley? Is there a prettier place in the United States?

We stopped for a snack. As we entered a small restaurant, the owner greeted us with a wide smile and said, "How are you doing today?"

"Does he know you?" I asked Nina as we took our seats.

"Everybody in America smiles and greets like that," she answered.

"Wow! He sounded as if he were waiting for you all day."

"Yes, he was," she laughed.

I loved her car. It was bigger than my bedroom in communalka, and the burgundy velvet seats were more comfortable than my living room couch. We arrived at a three-bedroom house with a fireplace that I could almost stand in. Peter, her husband, gave me a warm hug and happiness worked into my tired body.

The next morning, Peter asked me to go with him to buy breakfast food. First we bought fresh bagels in a bakery. How interesting! People did not stand in line. They took numbers and stood by the wall, not bothering each other. Cool.

Next we drove to a grocery store. I don't remember the name. It might have been a Kroger, but I do remember getting dizzy when I stepped inside. Peter took my hand. "Are you okay?"

"Yes, thank you." I tried to shake away my dizziness. I had never seen so many foods, so many beautiful-looking fruits and vegetables, so much of everything! I had found the answer to one of my questions about America: the streets were not paved in gold; all the gold was in the grocery stores.

"What do you want for breakfast?" Peter asked.

"Cheese and maybe some meat." My imagination could go no further than the rationed products of my country. Peter took me to various places in the store to find these items, and I was shocked to see at least twenty different kinds of cheese. I was accustomed to finding two varieties at most in Riga. I saw ten different choices of meat and hundreds of kinds of bread, muffins, rolls, buns, and so on.

I could hardly breathe. I was catching Peter's friendly and sympathetic glances. The last thing we needed was coffee beans. When we stepped into the coffee aisle, I came undone. I could not even count the many different kinds of coffee, teas, cookies, and chocolate bars. I could not help myself, and I started crying. I was thinking about my children, how they could not even dream of this pleasure. I thought about how in Latvia we had to produce food stamps for just the necessary things. We were always working, creating, building, doing, and shoving from one disaster, crisis, and temporary economic problem to another.

Now I wondered where all the products went that our people produced. The storm of these thoughts overwhelmed my mind. The Soviet government had been taking advantage of the great endurance and patience of our people for decades and decades.

Peter hugged me over the shoulders as I cried, and silently we walked away from the coffee aisle.

I liked everything in America! People were so friendly, smiling, and polite. That answered another question! I met Nina and Peter's friends, and we went to Japanese, Indian, Italian, and Mexican restaurants. We went to Jones Beach and to West Point, and then it was time for New York City. I'd heard and read so much about this city, and each personal experience of meeting the Capital of the World for the first time is different.

For me, I loved the lights of Manhattan. I liked the reflection of the sky in the mirror windows. I was surprised that such tall buildings, standing so close together, did not look heavy. They even looked fragile. Even those that were built in the 1930s made the same impression of readiness to fly.

Another strong impression was the smell, the aroma, of the places in New York. Actually, I enjoyed it everywhere in America. All the stores, restaurants, and homes smelled inviting. And the air conditioners! Wow. They were everywhere! We had very few air conditioners in Latvia.

I cannot forget my experience shopping at a small jeans store in Brooklyn. A gorgeous young girl worked there. She showed me all the fashions and styles, suggested I try them all on, and never disturbed me with questions until I wanted her help. She looked at me in each pair of jeans I tried on and ultimately helped shape my opinion. It seems a regular routine for me now, but then, a first-time visitor, I experienced a different level of human relations. It was not only an opportunity to buy better things in a better environment, it was a different feeling about myself through the considerate attitude directed towards me. Buying clothes in Soviet Latvia was still as personal as buying gas at a self-service station.

I spent almost a week in New York City. I stayed with my brother's friends who were new immigrants. It was their fourth month in New York and filled with problems that only immigrants know about: language difficulties, especially during phone conversations, a lack of money, and humiliation at using food stamps. Even though they were dentists and doctors in Latvia, they could not find simple jobs here because they were overqualified and did not have American diplomas.

Nonetheless, they welcomed me as a best friend. "We love your brother so much," they told me. "Of course, his sister will stay with us." They gave me their subway pass, and I rode all over New York City for a few days. It was an unforgettable time! Sometimes I would pinch my arm or cheek—was this real? Was I dreaming? Was I at the opposite side of the Earth in the greatest city of the world?

Yes, I was, and this feeling of exclusive reality made me smile. Wow, I was so lucky! I had found another answer to my question: in America, dreams are paved with gold. But I was also very homesick. I missed my children and the Professor.

Nina laughed at me. "Look at her, Peter. She is missing that bad guy!" They asked me if I wanted to immigrate to the United States.

"No," I replied. "Latvia is my home. I feel confident there. I don't care so much about the political situation or the economic conditions. It is my home."

Soon the month of the greatest adventure of my life, even more powerful than my Turkmenian adventure, was over. I was ready to go home.

The day before my departure, Nina and Peter surprised me with an offer. They said they had a laptop computer to give to my family. We could use it or sell it to somebody at home.

This confused me. I thought I had already received the most generous gift from them—a wonderful vacation. I could not accept another expensive gift. Personal computers, especially laptops, were very expensive in the USSR at that time.

"No, I can't really take such a wonderful gift."

"But you can sell it, and the Professor can buy a little house."

I did not believe he could, but I said quietly that if the Professor wanted to buy a house, he had to earn the money for it. Nina and Peter looked at each other and did not say anything else.

When the Professor met me in the Moscow airport, he asked if I had brought the computer.

"No," I said.

He said that was fine; he was asking just in case, because he had borrowed money for the custom fees from our friend. He did not make a big deal of my refusal of his sister's gift, thank God.

His meeting me in Moscow pleased me greatly. That same night we took the Riga-Moscow train and had a wonderful time. He talked about the kids, told me all they'd done together, and said he now understood how hard I worked at my job and at taking care of the family.

A warm and friendly feeling grew between us, and I marveled at the unexpected benefits of my New York vacation. Our relationship deepened overnight. I was happy with him again, and I could not wait to get home and hug my dear children.

"Thank you, America!" I thought. "You brought me back to my husband and my husband back to me."

Chapter Twelve

The Woman with Specific Style

> Marriage requires a special talent, like acting.
> Monogamy requires genius.
>
> — *Warren Beatty*

I was a girl with luck that ran backwards. Soon after I returned from my New York adventure, a new danger came into this world. If you saw her, you would remember her hair. She wore a specific style, a black pageboy that put a cute, sexy, sophisticated frame on a small face.

You know the sight of this woman with specific style. She typically has one overwhelming point of attraction. You might see it in the way she matches her scarves with her blouses, or her unexpected way of blending lipstick, or the way she confidently kisses your man at a party. She thinks she is special from birth, and she wants everyone to know it.

I met this woman with the pageboy haircut on New Year's Eve. Oh, it all started with the required amount of innocence. She was the wife of a long-lost friend who had bumped into the Professor in Riga in the afternoon. There was so much joy in this surprising reunion that the Professor had asked his friend and his wife and their little child to our place for a spontaneous dinner celebration of the New Year. I could see quickly that the Professor and the friend's wife liked each other. Their personalities flowed together like water into a dry garden. You will shake your head in wonder at my luck to learn that she was also a professor. I should have made a law for myself the moment she walked into my home: never trust a woman with specific style.

As my marriage trembled, so did my country. It was strange. Our country was still in the USSR, but thanks to *glasnost*, Latvia had made itself almost independent. The local Latvian government had opened the gates to private ownership and lifted the curtain for traveling abroad, and Western capital had flowed into the country. These same movements had blossomed in Estonia and Lithuania. For this reason, the reactionaries in Moscow ordered a military response to the Baltic reforms. Russian Special Forces attacked the communications and logistics centers in Riga. From our apartment, we heard the gun battle that raged for almost two hours. Ultimately, some Latvians were killed defending our nation.

I hated this violence. I had a friend whose son was in the Russian Special Forces. He told her all the boys hated shooting at their countrymen, but what could they do? They had to follow orders or eat their own bullets.

In March, the country had a vote about our connection with the USSR and almost everyone voted for real independence. At this time, ethnic Latvians, Russians, Jews, and other nationalities from across the Soviet Union living in Latvia were united. We all despised the Soviet system and believed nothing could be worse.

I was afraid our new economic and social freedoms would be turned around in a second. When this happened, I feared the guilty would punish the innocent. Can anyone forget Stalin's famous words? "Those who cast the votes decide nothing. Those who count the votes decide everything."

In the summer, the Professor and I rented a little dacha by the sea in Jurmala. The Professor had started his own training business, and he commuted back and forth to Riga. He also brought the woman with specific style into his company. You will find this hard to believe, given the shades of bitterness in my words, but at that time I was still innocent as to their relationship. They liked each other, but so what? After the queen had stepped from our lives, the Professor had stopped blowing his nose. But then again, the signs were clear to see: the Professor's new co-worker owned a dacha across the street from ours and decided to spend the summer near us.[4] This was one more proof of my hardest law: what can go wrong, will!

I have memories bitter and sweet of this summer. I picked blueberries with my children and made them jam. The blueberries by the Baltic are the best in the world. In the evenings, I took my kids to this other woman's dacha and watched *Good Night Babies* with them. Simon and Anna loved this show. All Soviet mothers of my generation will recall this program that helped us nurse our babies to sleep. It had puppets and lullabies and silly childlike dramas, and it played across the whole country every evening. During that summer, I liked it as much as the children.

As I have told you before, I loved to walk along the beach of the Baltic Sea. Sometimes, both families would walk. Usually my husband and the new woman would go ahead of us, engaged in important conversation about their work or writings. One time when I was alone with them, I became angry when they separated from me. I wondered if they would even notice if I left. I told them, "I'm getting cold and going back."

When my husband returned from this walk, he said, "Why are you demonstrating your emotions like that?"

"You didn't include me in your conversation," I replied. "You talked about things only known to the two of you. Do you think that your behavior is polite?"

"Why should we lower our conversation to your level? Don't you think you should come up to our level?"

His proud tone made me mad. "I don't think your level is so high," I replied. "It is just too boring for me."

---

[4] In Soviet times, one could own the dwelling on a piece of property, but never the land itself. It belonged to the state.

In August, the hard-liners started a coup against Gorbachev. Boris Yeltsin stood on top of an armored personnel carrier and defied those who wanted to turn back the hands of democracy. Yeltsin saved the day. This *putsch*[5] failed, and on August 18, 1991, Latvia declared its full independence. During this time, we heard that tanks were rolling up to Lithuania. In Riga, the patriots barricaded all the main streets with buses and trucks. Fathers built watch fires between the vehicles and slept in the streets to guard our beautiful city. Grandmothers, wives, mothers, and sisters brought courage and soup to their men.

I must admit I did not feel a strong role in this drama. It felt like a theater performance to me. How could these men stop real soldiers with guns and planes? Still, I respected them for their readiness to defend Latvia. Thank God, the tanks never entered the Baltics, and we turned to a new chapter in Latvian life.

When we returned to Riga later that summer, the other woman's husband called and asked me to meet him in the park. I liked V. He was nice, could laugh well, and he loved his family first.

"Do you know what's going on?" he asked as we walked on the path near the river.

"Not really," I replied. "What are you talking about?"

"Our spouses are in love. Are you blind?"

I wanted to say to him, "It's hard to open my eyes when I know I will see my own heart shut in my man's hand, when I know I will see the man deceiving me whom I have loved and still am in love with in spite of so many betrayals." But I could not say this, because I could hear the heartbreak in V.'s words.

"Of course they are flirting," I said.

"You don't know their games?" He cocked an eyebrow at me.

"No. I am not watching them. I keep my eyes on my children and my work. It keeps me busy enough." I didn't want to finish this conversation. My legs pulled me away from his words.

"When they go to their training retreats, they teach their classes together, and then they go into a room and have their relationship.

---

[5] *Putsch* means military overthrow of a legitimate government.

All of the students watch them come and go and understand their true natures."

"Oh." Now another sadness, as deep as any that I had ever felt about my marriage, grabbed me tight. The Professor had been bringing his students to our apartment for wine and good times. I loved to cook for them, to hear their praise for my borscht, to participate in their conversations filled with enthusiasm about the future. Some of you will know this secret hope that your man, by some miracle twist, has found pride in you. To hear that those smiling students knew my husband didn't love me was a most difficult eye-opener.

"Maybe we should have our own relationship," V. suggested suddenly. "This might give them some of their own medicine."

I smiled at his nice invitation, but I didn't take it seriously. This man I liked, and even if I knew then what I know now—that the woman with specific style would divorce him, that he would become an alcoholic, that she would block him from seeing his child and that he would die early and alone—I would not have given myself to him. I still loved my husband.

When we finished our walk, I went home and confronted the Professor in the kitchen. "Okay. I know you are having a relationship with her. She inspires your creativity and helps you become a better teacher. I can see how much your students appreciate your higher skills." Then, I went closer to him and reached to touch a button on his coat with my hand. I looked up into his eyes. "Don't let her go closer than this button."

"It is not what you are thinking," he said. "This romance exists only in your imagination."

"Don't make another orphan," I pleaded, thinking of how clearly V. loved his only child. "Don't let this one go deeper. If you stay on this side [meaning with me in the kitchen], you can keep her as a friend for life. As for the other path, if you take it, what should I do? How will I fly without wings?" I squeezed tight on his button.

"I will consider your thoughts," he replied. The conversation was over.

As I absorbed this new chapter of sadness in my marriage, my country was absorbing a new chapter of independence. I felt so sorry for my mom. The joy had completely left her. Have you ever built something—a relationship, a house, a family, a business—and watched it fall apart before your eyes? My mom had to watch her nation torn into pieces and then, just as quickly, she had to forget that Communism had ever existed. Even what was good from the Soviet system was pushed into the sewer. As if Communism had been only the slightest poof of history, Western air rushed into Latvia.

My mom's biggest fear before independence was that extremism would emerge, and this was soon realized. The united front of Latvian, Russian, and Jewish nationalities broke on the sides, the extremists came into the center, and they cried, "Latvians for Latvia!" But, who were the real Latvians?

The tests began. First, they tested our birth. If you or your parents were born in Latvia before 1940, citizenship was automatic. Thank God, I passed this test, but many did not. Imagine yourself in such shoes. Imagine your government declaring you a non-citizen tomorrow. How uncertain would you feel?

What would you think about your children, your social security? This exact measure of uncertainty fell on my best friend, Luda, who had been brought to Latvia as a young girl. I am glad she resolved this problem by going through a citizenship class that prepared her for a test on Latvian history and culture. Fortunately, she passed the test and again became a true citizen of Latvia.

Latvian officials also instituted a language test to ensure that Latvian would replace Russian as the dominant tongue. Although these tests did not impact citizenship, they put everyone in one of three employment classifications: #1, qualified for speaking with customers and citizens; #2, qualified for interpreting drawings and technical documents, and #3, qualified for solitary employment like cleaning offices or tending sheep. If your language skills failed to meet your job's requirements, you had to take classes and be retested until you passed. Those people who could not adjust were forced to find other employment.

I wish Latvia had granted citizenship to all her residents at the time of independence. Lithuania did so and avoided many arguments and tears. Though the tests were not unfair by themselves, to me they were unfair because many people who had to take them had spent their whole lives in Latvia. As you can imagine, these tests created much stress. Many Russians talked about moving east to their motherland, but they stopped mentioning this when their relatives sent word that life there was too difficult.

Quite simply, everyone was confused enough by independence without adding more stress. When I met with the tribunal for certifying my language test results, some words with a stiff spine came out of my mouth. "A person who was born in Latvia ought to have citizenship without any conditions," I said in perfect Latvian as I stood to leave. "Thank you, thank you, perfect," they replied, and into their chorus I threw the small smile of an independent woman.

And so, our little world spun from the bottom to the top. The Latvians made more laws to put their new edge on the Russians, and Russia heard the pleas of her exiled children and put an edge on the Latvians by cutting back oil shipments. As a result, bus and truck companies, including our TransInform customers, started their own spinning apart.

Through it all, the Professor maintained that I was only imagining his affair with the woman of specific style, until the day I had an urge to make blueberry preserves. You know how these sudden urges come into your body? It was the day my summer vacation was to begin. During my last hours of work, I decided to go home early and pick up some jars to take to Jurmala. Do you have a door in your house that remains always open? This door in my house was closed. I wondered, "Who would shut it? Is it the Professor's father? Why?"

I pushed open the door, and through the door on the other side of the kitchen, I saw the Professor wrapped in a blanket.

"I thought you were having beer with your friends. Didn't you say this to me on the phone?" I asked.

"I thought you were going to Jurmala?"

"I decided to make preserves." I walked into the living room and he stopped me from going further. What is this? I thought. Then, out of the corner of my eye, I saw a piece of woman's clothing on the floor.

"How nice! You can't even spend one day without a woman. Is it her?"

"Yes."

I imagined her hiding in the next room—our bedroom. A powerful anger came into my soul. In this moment, my love for the Professor began to run out of me as if a drain plug had been pulled from a lake. It would take a long time for the waters to empty, but sooner than I imagined, we would all taste mud in our hearts instead of water.

The Professor said he was sorry, but did he say he would stop? No.

I saw two unfinished glasses of beer on the floor. They tasted their fun in here before having sex in there, I thought. Suddenly, my feet kicked the glasses ever so gently to spill on the carpet. Let him clean up the mess.

I paid a price for my rude display. Two months later, in the fall of 1992, the rest of my luck surrendered: TransInform went out of business, and I was out of a job. Many of our customers went bankrupt, unable to make the shift from inefficient socialism to dog-eat-dog capitalism, and hackers with personal computers stole our applications and created much cheaper alternatives to our software.

Welcome to capitalism.

Chapter Thirteen

The Partisan's Daughter

Love is an ocean of emotions entirely surrounded by expenses.

—Lord Dewar

The plane flew from Roma to Riga too fast. I needed more time to shift back and forth the guilty feelings on my shoulders. It was the summer of 1996, and I was returning with my lover, Pavel (not his real name), from a weeklong secret getaway. Should I even tell this tale? Should I give such frank proof of a good girl gone bad?

Maybe it was my mom's fault for giving me dangerous courage. Or, maybe it was Gera's fault. He is Luda's husband. During a now long-ago visit, when Luda and I were discussing my marriage, he asked me what ingredients I put in my borscht.

"Why do you want to know?" I asked with surprise. "This soup has so many ingredients."

"Just tell me. You know how much I like your soup."

I smiled with the praise. I had always liked him. "All right ...I will try ... meat, hopefully beef, beets, carrots, potatoes, cabbage, onion, salt and pepper, tomatoes, a little sugar, sweet pepper, an apple, and greens like dill and parsley. What have I forgotten?"

"How much pepper do you put in your soup?"

"Of course just a little."

"So, put a little pepper into your marriage."

"What do you mean?"

"He means you should be a little bitch to him whenever you feel like it," said Luda, with laughter.

Gera had winced knowingly and nodded his head.

Yes, Gera can get the blame for this mess, I thought as I stared through the window into the sky across the face of Pavel, my handsome sleeping lover. Now there was too much pepper in the soup! In one Italian week in Riminni on the Adriatic Sea, I had fallen in love so deeply that a thunder had rolled into my heart and destroyed my fifteen years of marriage in a single strike of lightening. I couldn't forget Pavel's words when he saw me in the hotel lobby on the first day of our getaway. They transformed the contours of my self-image like a flood spreading the banks of a tired river.

"You look gorgeous!" he had said with deep feeling. Did he carry me into our cozy room? He could have. Did he undress every inch of me with his eyes before his first kiss? He might have. Did he make love to me like a man? Oh yes. When we finally completed our dance, I could barely walk or breathe. Ladies, have you ever had so much pleasure that you turned dizzy?

Pavel wanted me, and for one week, his wanting never settled or slumped or sagged. Trips to Florence, Venice, and Rome, afternoons at the beach near Riminni, evenings in the coffeehouses, hours in museums and antique stores, and gondola rides in Venice added to our pleasure.

My lover had the hard body of a lifetime soccer player. He was smart, too. His intelligence was obvious but not intense, so easy to breathe after years and years of the Professor's academic heaviness. He could name the birds in the trees as we walked to the beach. He also knew the names of most of the paintings we saw, as well as the artists, the styles, and the time periods in which they were painted.

I was not ready to return to Riga. I wanted to plan our next romantic adventure, but Pavel was sleeping. My happiness had been so short-lived, and now it was flying away from me at 500 miles an hour. My mind was on fire with one question: how would I return to normal life with the Professor? My lover had it easy. He was going to Riga to visit friends and then would return to America, where he now lived.

How did I know him? Pavel was a fellow Argonaut, one of my great buddies from my trip to Turkmenia in 1971. We were young then, and Pavel was sure of almost nothing except his desire to play soccer and cards, but when we went out in our group, he usually showed an interest in me.

Our relationship grew into something more after my dad died. Pavel saw my depression and called me often for walks by the river in the city or by the sea. I was not deeply in love, but his gentleness moved away my sadness.

One night he called and asked if I would like him to come over. My mom was away at a camp, so I asked him to stay and keep me warm. I don't remember much about this evening. To be sure, I didn't hear the strings of any sweet instruments. Was he all bungle and boiling with hot bloodedness? Perhaps. We were just kids, but I was happy to have him in my bed, and I didn't want him to leave in the morning. Some of you know this mix of feelings existing in these lands of friendship, love, and desire.

"Oh wow! What time is it?" he'd said when he'd finally awakened.

"It is time to get some coffee and a sweet roll," I'd replied lazily. "It is almost 8:00."

"No, I don't have time. I have to call my mother. She will worry about me." She didn't know where Pavel had spent the night, and when she didn't answer the phone, he focused on leaving as soon as possible. I couldn't hide my despair, and afterwards, I cooled down whatever feelings I had for him.

As the years rolled by, we occasionally met. It was easy. He lived near my TransInform office. I liked him, and we kept a casual friendship alive. He came to my wedding and heard the Professor's infamous response to Vladimir's toast. Many years later, not long before Latvia declared independence, he told me he was immigrating to the United States. I went to his good-bye party. He was married by now and everyone in his family was leaving—his wife, his daughter, his parents, even his brother and his family. Pavel walked me home. You might ask, "Where was his wife?" I asked the same thing, and he told me she had gone to another party. In his voice, I heard sadness.

At our good-bye, he promised to remain in contact, and then gave me a friendly kiss. I said, "*Derzhees.*" This means, "Keep yourself together" and expressed the hope that he would be okay, whatever happened in his new adventure.

I don't remember when he first called me from the United States. We talked in a friendly way. He told me about his immigrant troubles—finding a job, adapting to American ways, learning the language, helping his daughter in school, and so on. Maybe he called once a year, and then one year, he told me his wife had left him. The calls increased, and when the Professor openly continued his affair with the woman with specific style, I began to look forward to his calls. Pavel was a good listener and had a gentle voice for my troubles. One thing led to another, and he asked me to go to Italy with him.

"I am going on vacation," I announced to the Professor in the spring of 1995.

"Great idea! You deserve it," he replied with a smile.

He wants to be relieved from his guilt, I thought. In other words, "I'm still a piece of shit, but I care about my wife." Why did I stay with him in spite of his affair? Do you know what it is like to wear a pair of shoes that don't fit? Soviet women have a good knowledge of this. These ugly shoes pinch your feet and make you mad, but you don't want to put them away because so much time has been spent breaking them in. And, who knows what another pair will bring? Yes, even though my life didn't fit me, I had become accustomed to it.

"Are you meeting a handsome boyfriend?" the Professor teased not long before I left. Then he gave me some spending money. What an irritation! He knew I didn't have any money. Even though I now worked at a bank in the accounting department, I didn't make enough to go on a trip of this sort. He never asked me who was paying for the trip, but the first little drops of guilt fell on my soul. Was this his plan?

The loudspeaker came on, announcing we were cleared for landing in Riga, and my thoughts quickly came back to the here and now.

Pavel awakened and saw the high level of my nerves. "What is wrong?" he asked.

"Pavel," I replied, "my husband will pick me up. We can't get off the plane together."

He shrugged his shoulders, his way of showing he understood we had to pretend we didn't know each other.

When I saw the Professor and Simon waiting for me, a huge wave of guilt washed over me. The Professor held a bouquet of blue flowers, and Simon rushed into my arms with a wide smile. In one moment, any continuation of my affair with Pavel seemed impossible. I switched back to being a *mamochka* and made a picture of my life without him. Yes, I was ready to throw away all my pepper in two seconds!

Then, as we walked out of the airport, I saw a Latvian couple staring at me. Oh, my! They had been to Riminni, too. All week they had watched me loving Pavel, and now they were seeing another man meet me with blue flowers. I had not counted on tasting this shameful flavor in my soup, at least not so soon. My new law immediately became this: too much pepper spoils the soup!

The next day, a Wednesday, Pavel called and asked me to meet him after work. I had not talked with the Professor about what had really happened in Italy. Even today, he knows nothing, at least until he reads this.

Pavel and I met on a park bench and lit cigarettes.

"You look good," he said.

"I don't feel so good," I replied.

"What's wrong?"

"I lost my job at the bank today," I said. "Even though I've been at the bank almost two years, my boss had to lay off one person, and it was me because I have a husband who can still work."

I started crying, and Pavel and I talked a little about where I might find a job, for we both knew this was going to be very difficult.

The post-Soviet economy was terrible, and I had clung to that bank job as my life raft. Then I told him I had to go home. In the middle of the street, he stopped me.

"How is your relationship with your husband?"

We had not talked about my relationship with the Professor during our Italian hideaway. I hadn't wanted to. I'd thought, why put this stress into our affair? "Nothing special…We're just living together," I replied.

"You do have a choice."

"What do you mean?"

"Come and live with me."

"It is too late. I could never leave my children here."

"Come to America, to Detroit, with your children, and we will make a real family."

Chapter Fourteen

If You Don't Risk, You Won't Drink Champagne

All trials are trials for one's life, just as all sentences are sentences of death.

—*Oscar Wilde*

Women who have been married for a long time know when their men will become sick. The illness might come with dust and pollen in the spring or with the deep snows in the winter. When the illness arrives, we are ready with our kitchen-made cures and our warm voices, if we have enough energy for this sweetness.

The autumn was the Professor's unhappy season, so when he returned with a bad cold in October from a trip to Europe, I put him to bed and made my special inhalation from Siberian cider oil. It produces a healthy steam for opening the sinus cavities. After I placed it near his sleeping form, I returned to the kitchen, fixed tea with some balsam, and waited for him to wake up. I had something to tell him.

When Pavel left after our lover's getaway, I'd become absolutely stressed. After all, the day I'd returned from Italy, I'd placed my heart back into its prison of life without love. Then I'd looked at my hopeless situation, at nothing ever changing with the Professor, and I'd determined my fate.

Have you ever done this? Do you know this feeling of forcing your-self to look ahead for your children into the darkness? I had found a connection with someone I couldn't be with, but I had no connection with my husband. Then, this someone whom I had not seen for years, after one Italian holiday, suddenly offered his home to my two children and me. This generosity stirred my soul deeply, but I asked myself, "Who will take care of the Professor? Will this other woman do it? He is not getting any younger. And he has not too many friends."

Pavel called me from America and gently pressured me. "Will you come?"

For advice, I went to see my mom and brother. My brother and his family lived in my mom's apartment, along with our aunt. Independence had put an end to communalka, but not an end to the shortage of apartments for families like my brother's.

Three years older than me, my brother Jan is a mechanical engi-neer by training, a bank manager by profession. He is married to Valya, his wonderful wife from the Ukraine, and they have two daughters. He loves American jazz, good cigarettes, and a finely told sarcastic joke, but he looks at life from the shadows. What a man for finding the one thing that might go wrong with a plan, but you know, he gave me the money to go to Bulgaria with Ivar all those years ago. I have always looked up to him, but he has never looked down on me. Here is a story about him as a family man that shows his strength.

His second daughter was born under two kilograms (about 4.5 pounds), without reflexes. My brother and Valya scratched and hunted and begged for the best child specialist in Riga to treat this baby. The doctor sighed with the many demands on his skills, but answered my brother's pleas and examined the child. The doctor emerged from his work and gave my brother and his wife words that put a thickness into their dreams: "This baby is worth fighting for."

Valya stayed with the baby in the hospital for two months. Perhaps such care can happen in America, but I do not know of it. Then, the two parents centered their lives on making their daughter well. Today, this daughter is healthy and preparing for a rewarding life.

You must believe me when I tell you that my mom and brother did not know about my troubles with the Professor. They listened closely as I told them about the Professor and his queen, about their love child, and about this other woman he had been seeing for five years.

"How can you handle all of this?" said my mom. "I know that you do most of the family work and care for the kids while he runs his business adventures, but this other life shocks me."

I probably cried when more words came out. You know how it is. Then I told them about my trip to Italy and about Pavel and his offer to marry me and start a new family in Detroit.

"Detroit is the home of the carmakers," I said. "Beyond this, I only know that Pavel has his family and some friends with him. Will this make starting all over any easier? Who knows? Mom, what should I do?"

You can see that I didn't want to leave her. I wanted her to ask me to stay.

She gave me a thoughtful look. "If you trust Pavel, go to him."

How could she say these words so easily? "Mom, how about you? What will you do?" I cried.

"Your brother is here, and I'm here. My life is done. You can still find some happiness in your future." She was seventy-six and struggled with her health, but she had much to live for, or so it seemed to me. She had four grandchildren and loved to care for them, and she never acted in that irritating way: "Look at me and see how much I am giving."

But her face told me that the fire was almost gone. Was it the fall of Communism? The death of so many of her friends? This news from me? How could I ever be happy leaving her when she was only seeing her end? Nonetheless, the wings of this final chance beat in my heart on their own powers and flew me over my guilt.

"Mom, will you come and visit me?" I asked weakly.

"Yes, yes. I will visit you soon."

She will never visit, I thought, but I can go back home to see her.

"I think you have to go," said my brother. "If you stay, if you go back to the Professor, he will always make a rug of you and walk all over you. His whole manner of life upsets me. How could you live with these layers upon layers of betrayal? He is a man without a heart."

"I can't say exactly how I have lived so long with his ways," I responded. "I couldn't tell you about him. I wanted to let you know, but I worked so hard to get him inside the family. We could at least be together at occasions without arguments. If I'd told you about his other life, you would have had to make angry feelings disappear when you saw him. How could I put this stress on you, when you have your own heavy loads to carry?" I cried some more, and then finally asked, "Will he ever respect me?"

"No," they said together.

I left this conversation with less guilt but more sadness. My family was gently pushing my boat from the dock, but how could they let go of me, the one who truly knew them, the one they loved so much?

The great trial continued.

"Well, are you coming?" Pavel asked me over the phone.

"I want to come, but I'm not sure," I said.

"What are you not sure about? Family?"

"No, it is not them," I cried. "They support me as anyone knowing them would expect them to do."

"Then, the way is almost clear."

"No. I'm not sure yet if I can leave him alone."

"If you are not sure, then don't come."

I hate to admit it, but I heard a little click. Though overall Pavel was patient with my confusion, I felt that maybe he was already tiring of me, with my suitcases of doubt and worry.

Luda told me, "You have to make your own life, Asya. It's your chance to be with someone who loves you. Even if you get only one year of love from this relationship, it will be worth it, yes? Go, my best friend." She continued, "I can barely imagine living without you, but you know people are coming and going from Europe, America, and even Israel whenever they want. It isn't like yesterday, when your decision meant you left every friend and relative forever."

I thought of the Professor's sister. Nina had left Latvia in the 1970s with no hope of return. Thank God, I wasn't faced with that decision. Still, America meant nothing to me. Why did Pavel talk about America? How could I leave Riga? The streets were my family, and next to Luda, the cafés were my best friends.

I was raised in communalka. I didn't need separate living rooms and bedrooms. I didn't need grass yards with fences. I didn't need twelve shoe stores in one building. I didn't need a big career. I was sick. Sick with the feeling of hope, and the only hope for the rest of my life was to be loved.

Pavel, I can work hard, I thought. I can work three jobs. If I come to you, will you forgive my mistakes? Will you spend the rest of your life with me in gentle love?

Simon, who was now twelve, wanted to go, thank God. He hated his school and wanted to go to America. You ask, "Was it that simple to break a son away from his father?" You ask, "Did this son know the size of the break, the distance of the wound that would form?"

Not really, but these are my last words on the subject.

Anna said that she would stay with her father and come to America and go to the university after she finished her final year in high school. Naturally, she wanted to complete her demanding language arts program. She was already fluent in five languages, Russian, Latvian, English, French, and Spanish, and she will never forgive me if I don't mention that she also knew a little Swedish.

I wanted one more individual to judge this case, so I arranged to visit a friend who lived near the other woman's dacha in Jurmala who had known me for many years.

"I have a topic I want to discuss with you," I said after we shared our news of family and friends. We sat in a café sipping coffee as the autumn sun fell into the Baltic Sea. "But if my subject strikes you as too personal, please say to me, 'I don't wish to go any further on this.' I will understand completely."

"What is the topic, Asya?" he asked.

I blushed and turned my face.

"Come on. We are old friends. Out with it!"

"For years, we have come here in the summer and practiced friendly relationships with this family in a particular dacha. You know this family? Yes?"

He nodded.

"Have you seen my husband and the woman who owns this dacha together? Have you seen them coming and going when you would expect a husband to be home with his wife and two children?"

"Yes. Many times. In all seasons."

"Thank you." Then I told him of the decision facing me.

"Go," he said. "He will never stop, and with this betrayal he undermines all other trusts. Doesn't he? Even if it will not work—go!"

Dear Readers, that's what everybody told me: "Go!" It wouldn't have mattered if I were leaving for hell, as long as I was finally free of the Professor.

As I left my friend, a judgment settled in my heart. I wanted to live! Asya's Law: if you don't risk, you won't drink champagne.

Now, from the kitchen, I heard the Professor in the bedroom. I went into the room and helped him place the vaporizer against his mouth. While he began to breath in the cider airs, struggling against a heavy congestion, I sat in the swing chair next to the bed and began to talk.

"I have something to tell you," I said quietly.

"Oh?"

"I am going to leave you."

"What?" He put down the vaporizer and raised himself in the bed.

"I have met an old friend who wants to marry me."

"Wow!"

"I am going to America with the children."

"Why is all this coming out now?"

"You have your relationship. You have your life. You have taken my wings. What can I do? Where can I fly with you? I have no life with you anymore."

"We'll talk tomorrow," he declared, dismissing me as he had so many times before, but this case was not possible to dismiss.

"What is there to talk about?" I said. "You don't have any deep feelings for me."

Have you ever seen those little surveys in magazines that measure the stress level in your life? If I had taken such a test in the spring of 1997, I would have been off the scale. Many stresses collected on me at once, and they pressed on my chest like old bricks.

After I told the Professor of my plans to leave him, I still had to live with him. Yes, I moved out of our bedroom, but I tried to keep a normal environment in our home for the sake of the children. And, I have to give the Professor credit — he made the same effort.

I visited the Bureau of Marriage and applied for a divorce. We had a two-month waiting period before the hearing. Did we hire lawyers? No, they weren't necessary. We had nothing to divide, and we were in agreement that I would take the children to America. This agreement did not come easily. The Professor wanted to be sure that Pavel had the financial ability to care for Anna and Simon. Fortunately, Pavel provided the necessary proof of his income without one ounce of irritation. Pavel's attitude in this matter greatly increased my trust in him and in the future.

Dear Readers, you can probably guess the outcome, but the judge refused to grant us a divorce in the first hearing. She ruled that we had to continue in our marriage for six more months to try to fix our problems, even though we both stated that our marriage was over. From her judge's bench, she looked down at us and said, "I cannot divorce you so easily. You are still sharing householding."

As I listened to this judge, I felt a big frustration. The Professor had just publicly admitted that he had relationships with other women and that he agreed to this divorce. To me, it was absurd for the judge to deny our request. I did something that broke every rule of my obedient Soviet personality.

I jumped up and said strongly, "This is unfair! You won't divorce us just because we are sharing pots and pans?"

Wow! Did that ever annoy her!

"If you continue to speak this way to me, I will never divorce you," said the judge, and I fell apart into crazy tears. When I got home, I called Pavel and told him that I didn't know what to do. He suggested I hire a lawyer. Of course, I didn't have any money, so he sent some dollars with an American friend traveling to Riga. In a short time, I found my lawyer in the newspaper want ads, met him once to explain my situation, and he took my problems away. My angry judge granted my divorce on February 12.

But, there was no rest for me. I still had to organize my marriage to Pavel. I went to a different office of the Bureau of Marriage in Riga and applied for the permit, where I discovered that both parties had to appear for the application. Pavel couldn't afford to come to Riga for this procedure, wait for thirty days (the mandatory period), and then marry me. After some pleading, the Bureau allowed Pavel to mail his application from America. One more stress overcome! We set a wedding date for March 17.

Then, on February 23, in the middle of this craziness of managing divorce and marriage at the same time, my mother died. It happened so suddenly that for a long time I simply couldn't believe it. Later, I will tell you more about this terrible day, but as you can imagine, my mother's death deeply saddened and depressed me. I was also terribly lonely and overwhelmed with guilt. Did my plans cause my mom such pain that she simply couldn't go on?

I lost my excitement about going to America, but I knew I had to follow through on my plans. Pavel was counting on me, and the children were counting on me. Oh yes, Anna had changed her mind and had decided to come with me for her last year of high school. She and Simon had met Pavel and had fallen in love with him as he had with them.

Pavel and I had a very small wedding. Again, I married in the middle of the week at lunchtime. We had a short ceremony in front of a few close friends. For the second time, Luda was my witness. Later in the evening, we ate dinner in a cafeteria. We had a nice time, and Pavel spent a few days in Riga with me in an apartment that I rented for our honeymoon. Yes, I was still quiet from my mom's death, but this time with Pavel returned some of my hope for the future.

After our honeymoon, before Pavel left for Michigan, we applied for visas for the children and me to go to America. We had to wait six months to receive the necessary papers from the U.S. embassy. It was difficult and awkward living in the apartment with the Professor during this time, but what could I do? We couldn't afford to move to our own place, and we had to wait for the visas.

The Professor broke down once and pleaded with me to stay, but I told him he had made his own porridge and now he had to eat it.

"Is that new man of yours better than me?" he asked.

"To me, yes."

"You know what? Maybe you are doing the right thing," the Professor said.

I could not have agreed more, and on September 11, 1997, Simon, Anna and I left for Detroit.

Chapter Fifteen

After Seven Seas and Seven Mountains [6]

Everywhere immigrants have strengthened
and enriched the fabric of American life.

— John F. Kennedy

Pavel called his home a ranch. I am sure you know its style. It had one main floor spread over a square yard of grass and trees. Pavel, who had lived in an apartment before I came to the United States, had bought a new home for my children and me. When I was in Riga and he told me over the phone of his decision to buy a home in a good school district, I did not appreciate the concept. But, once in America, it did not take me long to recognize the many wonderful features of our school—the modern buildings, the sports fields, the computer labs, the good teachers, and the second language course for newcomers to help them step-by-step move into English classes.

My children liked their new schools! Is there a better feeling for a mother who has moved her children? In Riga, they had walked

---

[6] This is the traditional beginning of Russian folktales.

across the street to school. Here, they had to awaken at 6:00 a.m. to get ready for the bus, but it was easy to wake them up.

I quickly fell into the role of *mamochka*. I started each day by making the kids a light breakfast and lunch, and then did the same for my husband. I thought Pavel would like a different sandwich every day, so I tried hard to please him with a variety of meats and cheeses. A computer technician, Pavel spent his days driving between clients, and I tried to make it easy for him to eat in his car. I plucked grapes from their stems and put them in bags. I made his sandwiches small. I wrapped everything loosely. Before I left for work, I put his coffee on the table and walked into the bedroom, woke him up, and told him good-bye.

Ah, the memories! I had a great time that first Michigan fall of my life. Pavel's lifetime passion was soccer, and he played in a 40+ league. This team represented the United Nations. We had wonderful weekends at the games and at the parties afterward. My kids enjoyed themselves, and we met many nice people who understood firsthand our heroic journey and asked friendly questions about our homes, both old and new. These conversations helped me to start talking to people and reduced my fear of speaking English.

When these soccer players and their families congratulated Pavel for the brave decision to bring a wife with two children into his life, he seemed to swell with pride, and my sadness at leaving Riga flew away.

During my first year in America, I found a job as an accounts payable clerk in a construction company. Although I had spent seventeen years working with computer systems in Latvia, I had no confidence in getting similar work in America. I could hardly speak English, and too many years had been lost for me to keep up with the technology.

I could only count on the accounting skills I had gained during my last six years at home. Thank God, the owner of the construction company was also an immigrant. He understood the difficulty of my situation, how I had retrained myself to learn American bookkeeping, and how I struggled to learn English. I am grateful to this very moment for the chance he gave me.

Still, it was a challenge adjusting to the way of an American worker. It started with commuting. It took me three tries just to get my driver's license. The first time, I failed my parking test. The second time, the instructor told me gently that I was not ready and needed to practice more. Finally, I had my license, and though I drove fewer than ten miles to work, I had to forget about everything during this trying period two times each day.

I always felt like I was bothering people on the road. One guy would want to go faster behind me, but I couldn't go faster because I might miss my turn. Another guy would want me to pass through the yellow light, but I would always stop just in case.

Later, when my confidence increased, I started enjoying the greenery and the morning sunshine coming at me through the open landscapes. In Riga, the morning sun hid behind a fence of tall buildings, but in the U.S., it splashed its red energy through fields and between houses. I also liked talking to Jan and Luda. In my imagination, I made them sit next to me, and I told them this and that about America.

Do you see that big modern office building? Isn't it wonderful how they put flowers and trees around it and how they put benches in front so you can sit and smoke in the sunshine?

Notice how people care for their yards and fill them with bushes and fountains and tiny hills with rocks and birdhouses and gardens? See the large fields with green everywhere?

But why do Americans allow these ugly buildings? See that party store on the left? There it is, painted blue and yellow, placed between two modern office buildings.

Once at the construction company, I had other challenges. In Riga, I had organized my own time and worked in my own way, even during my time in the bank. My bosses did not control the details; I went to work and did what I thought needed to be done. My bosses had their rules and I followed them, but I had my little freedoms to keep myself human.

I could smoke when I wanted. I could walk across the street and get a coffee when I wanted. I could visit a friend in another department when I wanted. I could see a doctor during the afternoon without someone asking me, "Can't you go on the weekend?"

In America, it was very interesting to have my work steps so controlled by supervisors. For example, they would spend long minutes telling me how to put something in an envelope or how to put a number on a check: "Take this pen, instead of that pen, and put it exactly here every time, and don't forget that the boss likes to see it that way."

When it came to the big things about why we used this software or why we had to run that report, no one had an explanation. As a systems analyst, I liked to have conversations about why something was needed and how systems were shaped. This knowledge helped me to make decisions. In my construction company job and in every job I have had since, what I often hear is, "Don't ask me why. Just do it."

In my first months in an American office, I felt everything I did was watched and approved—going to lunch, taking a break, smoking a cigarette. I became guilty whenever I smoked, which took the joy away from me.

I learned the hard way about these rules. One day, I told my supervisor I had run out of cigarettes. I will go to the store for some, I told her. She did not reply, so I left. It took less than five minutes to drive back and forth from a nearby gas station, but the company owner, the wonderful man who had hired me, saw me pulling into the driveway. He waited until we were both in the office so everyone could hear him.

"What is the reason for you to come to work on time if you are leaving for fifteen minutes?" he asked in a very cold voice. He added, "And if you need cigarettes so much, why don't you buy them in cartons? You will save a lot of money."

He had never talked to me like that before. "Thank you for the advice," I replied politely, but in such a tone that everyone knew my stance: he had no right to yell at me for such a minor offense. The ladies around me looked in shock at the strength in my voice. Did they expect me to fall on my knees in tears? The lesson was hard for me to chew. I thought I still had my little freedoms. Now I understood that I had lost them.

Not that I was perfect. I put a burden on my co-workers with my poor English. Sometimes I felt their impatience as they watched me struggle to find the right words. During my first year in America, my worst experience was performing as the front desk receptionist. I had many troubles talking on the phone. It was humiliating to put someone on hold and ask a co-worker to speak for me. Yes, I had learned a little English in Riga, but it is one thing to speak in a class and another thing entirely to speak under the fire of a job.

I felt everyone was watching every mangled sentence, every mispronounced word. My thoughts were mostly correct, but my speaking sometimes came from another mouth. How could I say something so different from my thoughts? In my second year of work, I asked a friendly estimator this question: "Please, tell me the truth. Has my English improved at least a little since I came last year?"

"Honestly, I think it is at the same level."

Wow. It was tough to swallow his opinion, but I came to thank him many times for telling me the truth.

I enrolled in an English as a Second Language class at the local community college, and this helped a lot. I liked the atmosphere of the class. Young students and a young teacher energized me positively. I did my homework in the evenings and let Pavel examine me in learning new words. My co-workers respected my efforts and started correcting my mistakes. This was a good sign, because it meant they cared about me. I was becoming an American one sentence at a time.

Each day, after crossing the seven seas and seven mountains of learning how to speak English, how to work with Americans, and how to drive in crazy traffic, I turned my car into my neighborhood and firmly put my frustrations away. Another kind of test waited for me inside. Specifically, I had to learn about the importance of dinner.

The Professor had appreciated any food I made, but Pavel had certain preferences and expectations. Once I made chicken and rice, and he refused to eat it. Such foolish mistakes were never made by the Professor! Pavel wanted his mother's food, but it was too heavy for me. Besides, I hadn't learned how to cook as she did. She was a

Jew from Ukraine and I was a Jew from Latvia. In American under-standing, I was a Yankee and she was a Southerner: same nation-ality, different culture.

"Do you always cook with these sauces?" she would ask when I had made my famous goulash. Everybody in my family and all my friends loved it. "You have to learn my son's taste in this matter. You know, we like a real piece of meat. I'll help you!"

You women know these conversations with your mother-in-law, especially one who is too often raising her son after he has become a man. Asya's Law: listen to your mother-in-law, agree, and then do it your own way.

After dinner, the children sometimes watched television with us, but mostly they went to their rooms and did homework. Anna wanted to go to the university and put many, many hours into this dream. Would you believe that she scored over 600 points on her verbal SAT four months after taking that eight-hour plane ride from Riga? As for my baby, Simon, he fell in love with computers and eventually built his own machine.

My relationship with Pavel came alive after the kids went to bed. He was consumed with collecting. He bought books, pictures, and paintings and spread them like a flood over the house. Every wall except the bathroom was covered with pictures. There was not even room for my favorite painting, the only picture I had brought from Riga. I hung it in the laundry room in the basement.

Books were piled on the floors, in the corners, and under the stairs. At night, we worked together putting books in order and dis-cussing his new purchases. He went on eBay searching for new pieces of art while I read and wrote letters to my friends. Around eleven, we had tea and bagels. I always made sure he had the dark Hershey's chocolate that he loved.

And, not long after midnight, he often made sure that the fire-works in Michigan were as strong as the fireworks in Italy. Yes, I always expressed excitement about his king-sized bed. I could roll over twice and not fall off.

Chapter Sixteen

You Cannot Read a Stranger's Soul

There is always a spoon of tar in a barrel of honey.

—Old Russian Saying

When it comes to moving to a new home, Russians have a cute superstition of allowing a cat to step in first for good luck. So, before I left Riga, Luda gave me a stuffed white cat. I loved this cat. It hugged me whenever I was lonely, even though it did not get to step first in the house—the honors and luck went to Pavel and his mother, who made up the home for us before we arrived.

Yes, they set their luck first. Maybe this was why a darkness started to form underneath our happiness. The first trouble came shortly after we arrived, when Anna and Simon were raking leaves under the supervision of Pavel and his mother. While my new family collected leaves, I fried pork chops, one of Pavel's favorite meals. Suddenly, Anna ran into the kitchen.

"Mom, I think I did something terrible." Her face was confused and red.

"What happened?" I asked, immediately concerned.

"I said something to Pavel's mom."

"What did you say?" My knees felt ready to slide to the floor. I didn't want anything to spoil our fairy tale. I have to admit that I really wanted Pavel's mom to like me. I had felt a couple of clicks that made me believe we had major differences, but my goal was to overcome them. Then Anna told me what had happened.

"When we were raking the leaves, Pavel's mom said that Simon left a lot more leaves unraked than me. I told her that our mom never compared us when we were doing something together. She got mad at me. She made an angry face. What should I do?" Anna was seventeen years old and always quick to protect her brother.

"Thank you for defending Simon and me, but I think you have to apologize," I said.

Anna quickly agreed and ran outside to say she was sorry.

Five minutes later, Pavel walked into the kitchen with a pale face.

"What happened?" I asked, further frightened. I remember his answer as though I heard it this morning.

"Your daughter just gave a lecture to my mom on how to raise children."

"But she apologized?" I asked with hope in my voice.

"I don't know," he answered.

Dear Readers, I trusted that Anna could straighten out this situation, but I was wrong. Pavel's mother did not return to our house for six months, and this first trouble turned into a deep conflict between the two of them and, eventually, me. Slowly, Pavel and his mother put Anna into the shade of the family. I tried to make peace and to keep the light on Anna, but I failed.

Anna was a special girl. She had an adult attitude about our family dynamics, and she kept a deliberately positive and supportive relationship with her father. She wrote him regular letters and called him, for she understood his loneliness and sorrow about losing us.

In Pavel's home, she tried to be a good girl—no loud music, no messes, no long telephone calls, and no angry slamming of doors. On the contrary, she focused almost completely on her studies. Her only sin that I could see was that she was not extroverted enough for Pavel and his family.

Pavel demanded an unusual kind of respect for giving Anna a roof and food. For example, he wanted her to leave her room when he walked in the door from work and greet him with a cheerful face. Her own father didn't have these lofty expectations, but this style is common in some stepfathers, isn't it? They want a perfection they cannot get from their own children. Pavel had a teenage daughter who visited often, and she could easily lead him by the nose whenever she wanted to.

What was Anna's problem? Pavel's mother thought she knew the answer. She told me that Anna was a good girl but had too much honor for herself and her intelligence. Pavel himself said that Anna thought she was the smartest person in the world. He actually said "world," and whenever I asked for advice, he would tell me, "Go to your best advisor," meaning Anna.

Things worsened between Anna and Pavel our first summer in America, when the Professor sent Anna and Simon money to return to Latvia for a visit. Pavel didn't want them to go.

"Nobody goes back so fast. They should be working and making contributions here," he said.

For me it was easy to understand—their father missed them; they missed their father. They were only going for a couple of weeks. Why not? I thought. Did Pavel want them to end their relationship with their father so he could think he was on top?

Pavel accused me of giving Anna his money so she could make the trip. Even then, it struck me that he didn't have the same concern about Simon.

"I want to see her bank statement," he insisted.

Anna was furious, but we showed him how the bank had accounted for a transfer from the Professor. Pavel's laws of ownership were becoming clear: everything was his, and nothing was mine. Also, I felt deep disappointment—he did not trust me! The children bought their tickets and went anyway.

Unlike many teenagers, Anna did not ignore the conflict between herself and Pavel. It caused her deep pain. She loved and trusted Pavel, but her faith in him was beginning to dissolve. On the other hand, she felt guilty about making him angry and hurting my chance for happiness.

I will never forget the day during our first year when the conflict reached critical mass. Pavel lay on the couch, watching TV, while I sat on a nearby loveseat. Anna came into the room, sat on the carpet, and began talking. Here is what was said:

"Pavel, can you explain to me what I am doing wrong? Why are you so mad at me?"

As she spoke, I moved to the edge of the loveseat. I didn't know what to expect.

In a cold, indifferent voice, without turning his face from the TV, Pavel said, "I am not mad at you."

But he said this in a bored, disinterested manner that sounded like "I don't care," and my heart sank into despair.

Anna continued to ask him to explain what she was doing wrong. "I don't want to spoil everything." Her voice shook and tears rolled down her face, yet he still refused to turn his eyes to her as she sat below him on the floor. Unable to take this worst kind of punishment, Anna fled to her bedroom, and soon I heard her sobbing.

I went to her and saw her sitting on the floor, writing hysterically on a piece of paper. It was a letter to Pavel, and I still remember the first lines: "I don't know how this could happen. I love you. I just can't stand it anymore."

My sorrow for Anna poured from me, but I let her write without interruption as my heart beat like a rabbit running from a hunter. Then we looked at each other, she put down her pen, and we hugged.

"It is not your fault," I said.

I left Anna's room, composed myself, and approached Pavel, who was still watching TV.

"Do you have a heart of stone? How could you watch her crying and ignore her like that?" I asked him. He shrugged his shoulders, showing that there was nothing to talk about.

Everyone had told me how much Pavel loved children. He was a sensitive and loving father to his daughter, who was two years younger than Anna. I had seen him many times on the soccer field, helping kids learn to play. As I said before, Anna and Simon fell in love with Pavel on their first meeting in Riga. I couldn't understand why he was so tough and unforgiving with Anna. I didn't know this side of him. I realized with a shock that he was still a stranger to me. So the new law I took into my heart was simple: you cannot read a stranger's soul.

After that, whenever I saw the white stuffed cat Luda had given me, I remembered that this good luck charm had failed. I couldn't help but ask myself, "Is there any luck for me here?"

Chapter Seventeen

To Go Or Not to Go?

People change and they forget to tell each other.

—Lillian Hellman

It was Thanksgiving Day, 1998, shortly after breakfast. After fourteen months in America, I still felt like a stranger, even in my husband's home. I sat by myself on a couch in our careful living room in our quiet suburb of Detroit. This silent place seemed to me to be without life. It was nice and green, but there were no children in the yards and no parents on the streets. The only place to walk was to your car, where you would be taken somewhere, away from the neighborhood. Riga's crowded streets had never seemed more inviting, and I was filled with longing for my old home.

I sat alone, trying not to disappear into the cushions, stressing over Pavel's questions.

"Are you going with me to our family dinner?" he had just asked. "Or should I tell my mother that you and your children are leaving our family?"

Our relationship, constructed so painfully on our faith in our powers to build a new family out of two broken ones, had fallen apart, piece by mysterious piece, until only his two questions remained as the foundation: "Will you stay? Or will you go?"

Dear Readers, you can imagine how I shook on these cracked branches of our dying love. Thank God, Pavel gave me time to think and did not yell. For once, he didn't put more guilt on my shoulders, only the questions.

The heavy load of having to answer him pressed on my chest. I could hardly breathe. I could hear my heart beating like crazy. What should I do? Was there any chance left for Pavel and me? Could we stay in America if I left him? Would the immigration service send us back to Latvia? Would I have enough money to support us?

With my side vision, I noticed Simon looking at me from the hallway. He had heard Pavel's questions, and knew what they meant. When I looked at him, he quickly disappeared into his room. He was scared.

Until recently, Simon had escaped the shade that had imprisoned Anna. Pavel and his mother had favored Simon. He was quiet and polite, a classically introverted boy who stuck to his studies. Sometimes Pavel blamed him for laziness, but Simon never refused to help around the house when asked. However, all this changed for Simon as the first year progressed. I remembered how it started—over strawberries.

One day that summer of 1998, a friend and her daughter visited, and I bought two quarts of wonderful Michigan strawberries for the occasion. Pavel, our friends, and Simon and I sat around our patio table drinking coffee and eating cookies. Everyone was in a good mood when I placed the strawberries in the middle of the table.

As we began eating the strawberries, Simon began devouring them one after another. No one seemed to care about Simon's appetite except for Pavel. I noticed a yellow light in his eyes as he watched the juicy red berries disappear into Simon's mouth. Pavel didn't take a single berry, and I knew trouble was ahead. I wanted to stop Simon somehow, but I couldn't say a word. I didn't want to embarrass him.

Later, when our friends left, Pavel said, "Simon ate almost all the strawberries himself."

"Why didn't you eat any?" I asked in a tone that indicated it didn't matter that Simon had eaten so many. "Tanya and Masha ate them, as much as they wanted. Why couldn't Simon do the same?"

"Maybe I wanted to eat them later. He doesn't think about anybody but himself," said Pavel.

I reflected on Pavel's comments. Objectively, he was partly accurate. Simon was not a baby. He could have thought about saving some of the strawberries for others to eat. On the other hand, Pavel was also acting like a baby, building up steam over a trivial sin and spoiling a warm and satisfying event.

Nonetheless, I talked to Simon and cautioned him about eating so heartily of Pavel's food. Yes, I said "Pavel's food," as it was now clear to me that Pavel had drawn a line between himself and Simon.

It wasn't just his relationship with my children that had gone wrong, though. Pavel had begun to find fault in me. It began with one question that grew like a weed into a hundred questions, none of which I could answer to his satisfaction.

One day I called Luda to get a copy of my diploma from the university for a curriculum evaluation by the local college. Because Riga is seven hours ahead of Michigan, I called her early in the morning from the basement. I didn't want to bother anyone's sleep. Luda wasn't home, so I left a message with her aunt.

The next day, out of nowhere, Pavel asked me, "Why did you call somebody from the basement?"

I had almost forgotten about the call, so I replied, "What call?"

"Early yesterday morning, you called somebody from the basement. Who did you call?"

I told him I had called Luda and explained the reason.

"But you didn't talk to Luda."

"I talked to her aunt."

"Okay, but why from the basement?" he asked. His tone implied, "I will accept a version of your story for now, but I am not really satisfied."

"I didn't want to wake anyone up."

"But why did you do it from the basement? Didn't you know that I can hear everything from the house?"

"I didn't know that," I said and I ended the conversation, leaving him with his dissatisfaction.

Once I saw the following statement on a T shirt: "The beatings will continue until morale improves." Eventually, I came to realize that Pavel wanted to prove I had a secret life behind his back, and that is why he kept asking me questions.

"Why don't your friends talk to me when they call?"

I didn't know, but after several rounds of this discussion, I humiliated myself by calling my friends and family and asking them to say a few words to Pavel whenever they phoned.

How did the happiness of Pavel's big bed turn into such a mess? Even today, I do not know exactly how it happened that I lost my friend, my lover, and my husband. Somehow the whole relationship trickled through my fingers, and the tighter I squeezed, the more I lost.

I think it must have started when we got off the plane, only this change I did not immediately see. Probably I felt it deep down inside, but I thought it was an adaptation period. I wanted to make a new family so badly that I did not choose to recognize what was probably staring me in the face.

Ultimately, Pavel came to believe that I was selfish, pragmatic, unnatural, weak, and snobby. In all my years with the Professor, he had never complained about my character. Oh yes, he made stupid comments about my intellectual interests, but when it came to character, he held me up as the ideal of Russian, Soviet, Latvian, and Universal motherhood and wifehood.

"Why did you open your bank account in the same branch as your daughter did?" Pavel asked once.

I had opened my account at a neighborhood bank within walking distance. My very first job in America was at a drugstore near our home, and I wanted to deposit my little check by myself. I had asked Pavel to advise me on the best bank, but he had taken forever to make a decision, so one day I just did it. In return, Pavel accused me of wanting a different bank than his. I couldn't bring up the energy to argue this point. Could you have?

Dear Readers, here is the big picture: as I failed to respond to Pavel's questions to his satisfaction, he became tougher on me. Each night in our bedroom, I encountered a man I did not know, an angry man, a man of stone, a bookkeeper of my faults. As I became more tense, he felt more and more like a stranger to me. Of course, he noticed my anxiety and blamed me for acting as a stranger.

As you have probably guessed, I tend to blame myself first for any of my relationship problems. Of course, Pavel knew this aspect of my personality and only made things more difficult for me by asking, "Why are you always afraid to do things wrong?"

This question created a double guilt—one for being guilty and another for being afraid to be guilty.

This chain reaction put me into total confusion and locked me into a prison of the mind. I tried to get out with a poem I wrote for Pavel called "Still Life."

Still Life
Please give me a hand,
Please look at my eyes,
It's the only way
To make me be nice.
What can I do?
No second life for me.
I shall transfer for you
Into a still life.

I'll be a vase,
I'll be a fruit,
I'll be a nut.
And then what?
You'll look at me,
You'll bring me home,

Maybe you'll make
For me a new frame?

Maybe you'll put
Me in a new place,
Maybe you'll paint
Over me a new vase,
A new fruit,
A new nut.

But no second chance,
Even for us,
We have to keep
All that we have.

When Pavel finished reading my poem, he made no comment on its meaning, only asked, "Why in English?"

Many of you ladies will recognize this short, non-feeling response from a man. However, you will also know that I couldn't quit trying. Our female character is our destiny.

My evolving relationship with Pavel reminded me of a story I'd heard about Christopher Columbus. When he arrived in America and anchored his ships in the Caribbean, the Indians did not see his three ships, even though they looked at them in the harbor. They looked, but they did not see. Only when the shaman came and said, "The gods have come here" did the Indians realize that something very new had happened in their lives.

I simply had no experience in this kind of war, and Dear Readers, as you well know, I had no muscles, not even one, for yelling, screaming, and getting red all over my body. My only response was to keep trying to prove to Pavel that I loved him and that I wasn't a bad person.

Nonetheless, on occasion, I couldn't help but wonder if maybe there was something wrong with Simon, Anna, and I after all.

Maybe I had come from a bad family. Maybe my parents had made mistakes that I could not see. Maybe I was a bad mother.

How could I have these insane debates with myself? I don't know, but I did. Pavel's and my love had become a balance sheet, and I was always in the red. Soon I spent every day, every minute, talking to him in my mind, explaining why what I did was not what he thought it was.

"You complain that I put you in the last place. You are in the first place," I said one day. "For example, when I am doing the laundry or ironing, I always start your clothes first."

"Yes," he said. "The laundry. Why don't your children help more with the laundry?"

Many times I asked my Latvian loves, Luda and my brother, what to do. What did they think? Why didn't Pavel like me anymore?

At the beginning, they told me it was temporary, that we were simply having a hard time getting used to our new life. But then they started worrying about me.

"Nobody has the right to humiliate you," my brother finally told me. "Listen, nobody—not a husband, nor co-workers. Get back to yourself. Like you were before the Professor. This is the only way to save yourself."

Shortly after that, on a nice September night, Pavel and I came home a little drunk from a party and made love. I admit that his touches made me hopeful. The next night, I was showing him signs of my love.

"Don't think my softness from last night means that all is right," he said coldly.

"Do you know what a woman has to do after hearing these words?" I asked after a minute of confusion and the pain of rejection.

"What?"

"Go away and never come back."

Pavel's and my relationship was now so bad that I placed a deposit on an apartment near Simon's high school. Anna had already graduated from high school and was in college. Pavel knew about the apartment, and I hoped that a short separation might lead to a long-term reunion. So, when he asked me if I was coming with him to Thanksgiving dinner, he was also asking me, "Are you really moving into this apartment on December 1?" Now I will tell you why I pushed back all my unhappiness and confusion and decided to stay.

I wanted to stay with Pavel for my children. I believed that Simon would feel more secure in a family situation than he would with a single mother. Even though he found himself in Pavel's shade, he liked the broader family that had come to America so long ago with Pavel—the cousins, the aunts and uncles, even Pavel's mother. As for Anna, I knew she wanted to escape Pavel's house, but if I left, even for a short separation, I risked not getting permanent residence status—i.e., my green card. It was a sign of my great frustration and unhappiness that I seriously considered leaving Pavel when the hazards were so great.

If Pavel and I divorced before I had been in the United States two years, there was no chance of getting a green card because the Department of Immigration and Naturalization Services would assume that I did not come to America to live a family life and the children and I would be sent back to Latvia. This is why Pavel and I talked temporary separation and not divorce, but I was still afraid even of separating. Although I would have been fine returning to my lovely Riga, my children had already put their destiny into America. Neither of them wanted to go back to Latvia. Ironically, even though they suffered under Pavel, I had to stay to give them a better future.

Also, to be wholly fair, I recognized that Pavel was suffering, too. Adapting to a new family was hard for him, and I did my best to put myself into his shoes. The woman he had fallen in love with and her two teenagers had been very nice and easy-going back in Riga, but they had suddenly fallen down on his head with their own habits, characters, differences, and necessities. There is an American saying: marriage is a tango for two. I knew that some part of our unhappiness must come from my personality. I, too, was having problems adjusting to America and this new family.

Pavel was right. I was tense, and I became too upset at any little mistake I made. It was also difficult being so financially dependent on him. The Professor and I had been relaxed in money questions, but Pavel's attitude towards money was argumentative. He expected a justification for all expenditures, and he expected me to offer all my money to him. Now you can see why he counted the fact that I had opened my own bank account as a betrayal.

On that Thanksgiving Day, I also decided to stay because I saw some reason in his expectations and some hope that I could adjust to meet them. Like a tree on a large rocky cliff, I dug my roots into the stone.

The conversation Pavel and I shared the day before Thanksgiving also made me wonder if some kernel of love remained in his heart. I didn't know how to reach this kernel, but the fact that it might be in him raised hope in me.

"Maybe we can try again," he had said. "It won't be easy for me. I don't promise anything more than my efforts, but I am willing to do this."

In the end, I decided to work on myself. Asya's Law: if you want to change someone else, change yourself first. After thinking through the situation for several hours, I became convinced there was enough hope between us to justify one more try. I got up from the couch, went into the kitchen, looked into Pavel's eyes, and then the final decision came from me: "I want to stay with you."

"Good," he said, giving me a smile and a hug. Simon, who had been waiting patiently in his room for this conclusion, came into the kitchen, saw our hug, and smiled with relief.

Chapter Eighteen

The Last Drops of My Patience

A mother's treasure is her daughter.

— Catherine Pulsifer

There is an old Russian saying, "You cannot make the broken cup whole again." You can glue the separate parts together, but the cup will still be broken and will shatter with the smallest pressure.

So it was with Pavel and me. Our cup couldn't be restored. Despite our work, peace and warm relationships stayed in our home only for a short time and then flew away. The pressures of our unhappiness returned. Pavel went back to the old questions and created some new ones, and I was still unable to answer them to his satisfaction. He even worked harder to find faults in me.

Here is an example. Once I bought some things for his mother without telling him. She and Pavel were going on a vacation to Spain. Our relations had become so cold that Pavel thought it was natural to go with his mother on this kind of vacation without me.

I was trying not to make a big deal about this fact. I even looked forward to two weeks without Pavel as my own vacation. So, with this feeling in my heart, I bought his mother a beach bag, shorts, and a blouse for the trip. I'd told Pavel I was going to shop for some nieces in Riga, but when I arrived at the store, I changed my mind and shopped for his mother. She was picky, and I thought I'd found some items to fit her taste.

When I showed Pavel my purchases, he became irritated. "You told me you were shopping for your nieces. Why did you lie to me?"

"Why do you treat me this way? Am I that bad?" I asked in return.

"Yes, you are. Because you don't do anything good," he said. "And even if you do, you are doing it in an unnatural way."

These words made the last drops of my patience evaporate. Ironic, isn't it? The first click I'd ever felt with Pavel so many years before after our summer in Turkmenia and the last click I felt now were both related to his mother. Though indirectly she was the source of our unhappiness, I cannot blame her. Pavel was the one who asked me to come with my children to America to build a new family, and he was the one who decided not to keep this family around him.

As time went on, I tried less and less to keep the pieces of our relationship together, and the pressures increased for all of us. Simon became silent and retreated more often to his bedroom. Luckily, Anna found the love of her life and spent increasing amounts of time with him. Almost a year after my Thanksgiving decision, Jeff asked her to live with him, and she agreed.

Her departure made a huge impact on me. It saddened me, it thrilled me, and it inspired me. I was happy that Jeff had wrapped her in so much love. I knew my girl, my little-big-smart-brave girl. Even though she was mostly a silent witness, I always knew she suffered with me. I knew she felt deep pain for me, deep regret that everything had turned upside down. As I began to work through the decision to leave Pavel for good, I realized that my daughter was showing me the way to freedom.

Our home became even quieter after her departure. No, it didn't make one thing better between Pavel and me, even though I am a little ashamed to say I hoped it might.

I missed Anna terribly. I began talking to her in my mind about my situation, and I heard her voice guiding me. She became one of my strongest supports. Her speech in my mind was such a powerful help that I decided to put her words into an imaginary letter to me. Anna has seen this letter, and she agrees that it reflects what she felt and thought.

June 12, 1999

Dear Mamochka,

Although I am only nineteen years old and just opening a new chapter of my life by moving in with Jeff, I wanted to write you about my feelings. Mom, I have not left Simon and you because of Pavel. I wanted to be with Jeff and his daughter. I know it has been hard for us to talk in the last year and that I went months without saying more than five words. This letter will overturn some of my silence.

When I first met Pavel in 1997, I thought he was the opposite of Dad. He was loyal, attentive, down-to-earth, and did not have Dad's stuck-up intellectual attitude. Dad never tried to hide his infidelity from you or us. First, I thought you deserved more. Then, I thought we deserved more.

When Pavel came back from your past and from America and you told me about your history together and his desire to have you forever, I thought it was really romantic. For years you lived different lives across the oceans. He kept love's flame alive and returned across the waters to rescue you.

I know it took me a while to decide to come with you to America. I was worried about Dad. Who would take care of him? That was soon answered, when the woman with specific style moved in with him. So, I decided to come to America with Simon and you. It was the right choice then, and it is the right choice today.

When did things go wrong with Pavel? From the first day! As soon as he picked us up at the airport, he stopped talking. When he did talk, his words came through a tunnel. I felt an immediate chill. Of course, we were withdrawn ourselves. It was quite natural, given the scene we had left at the airport in Riga. I can still see Dad's face. It was three inches longer than usual, and so pale! He was a broken man. Did he beg you to stay the night before? Was it hard to refuse him?

I remember that I was waiting for my classmates to arrive at the airport for a final good-bye. They were late, and you were falling apart while at the same time consoling Dad. You hugged him and kept repeating, "You will be okay! You will be okay!" Mom, you said it so many times I knew you didn't believe it.

Then it was time to go to the gate. I broke into hysterics on the inside, but I didn't show a thing as I silently followed you, so sorry to leave Dad, so sorry not to say good-bye to my friends.

From the moment we landed, we wanted Pavel to lead us. In the beginning, there was hope. Pavel drove us around the state, showing us the best places, local lakes, and cities. It was fun, really, and you both looked so happy. Remember, I told you once, "He really loves you!" And you asked me, "Why do you think so?" I told you, "I can see it by the way he opens and closes the car door for you."

Oh, I was so young! Is it possible to age fifty years in two? I can write a paper about it if you want. How could it all change so fast? Poor Grandma. If she were still alive, she would die twice – first for seeing what he did to you, and second for seeing what he did to us. He abandoned us in America. How can you forgive a man who does not speak to us for months on end? Not one word for four whole months. And for what? Because we wanted to go back to Latvia to visit Dad?

You blame yourself for this mess. You still put yourself on trial. Why punish yourself? Get out before he drives you totally crazy. You did not turn him against us, and you did not turn us against him.

It is time to stop crying – for Dad, for Simon, and for me. Especially for me. I am glad to be in America. I am headed to a university to pursue my dream of becoming a teacher. I love this country – its size, nature, people, and opportunities. I think you are even starting to like it. Thank you for bringing me here, and always remember, when you are ready, Jeff and I will help you to get free.

Your Loving Daughter,
Anna

As I finished this letter, a powerful, unexpected desire came up inside me. I wanted to feel like a daughter again. I needed my mother, and I wanted to talk to her. The memories of her last days overwhelmed me, and I wrote another letter, this one to her.

Dear Mom,

I remember every detail, every moment, of the night you died. It was a month before my marriage to Pavel. I came over as usual on Sunday to visit you. When I stepped into your room, I found you on the floor. A cigarette, your last one, was lying nearby. I can't remove that cigarette from my mind. The ashes were scattered on the floor away from the end, like your life, I guess. You weren't breathing, but I thought I could hear your pulse, and I yelled for Jan to get an ambulance.

This time the ambulance men did not climb to the sixth floor. They took an elevator, but nothing could be done for you. They told me that the pulse I felt was my own. I felt my life in your death. How could such a thing as your death happen? You were supposed to live forever.

We asked the old and tired ambulance man, "Why did our mom go?"

He looked at us in our grief and told us, "It was her time. Just an age."

It is so difficult to remember those defeated words. As I looked at your gentle, silent body, all the times of our lives sifted down and through the hourglass with no chance to gather them and resume life for a day, for an hour, for just one moment. I miss you so much.

I can still see your eyes. I can hear your careful words as we discussed my future plans. How deep was your pain because of my leaving? You never showed any sign. You protected me from guilt. Only a person with a huge heart could make such a gesture. I know another person who could do it: Dad. How could we live without him for so long?

Your funeral day was a typical Baltic winter day – cloudy and gray. We did it in the Jewish tradition. Why? Who knows. Maybe the following story explains everything.

Everybody was in the temple. The Rabbi read a kadish. A violinist played a wonderful movement from Greig. To the roof, the Rabbi's words floated, together with the sounds of Greig's haunting music. I raised my eyes to the windows under the ceiling, and I saw a strong wind chasing away the clouds. Then, a bright, unforgettable blue sky opened up and poured sunlight into the temple.

The sky opened for your soul, Mom.

Sometimes I dream about you. One dream I cannot forget. We were at the beach. You and I went inside the bathhouse to change. The bathhouse turned into a labyrinth, and with your help I struggled to find my way out. I finally emerged by myself. Then I woke up. You had helped me find a new path, and your voice was clear: "Take care of yourself."

Thanks, Mom.

Your Loving Daughter,

Asya

The process of writing these letters to the two women I love so much helped me to forgive myself for staying with Pavel and enduring his abuse. It also helped me to know what to do next. All my agonizing was gone, and I knew that enough was enough.

In August of 2000, Simon and I finally left Pavel and his home and moved into a one-bedroom apartment. I gave Simon the bedroom. Teenagers need a place to study and for their privacy. I slept on the couch in the living room, and I slept well! For the first time in years, nobody was watching how I was standing, turning, cooking, or spending money. I felt a quiet happiness to be by myself with my son.

I found the best lawyer in the world to help me file for divorce, and you know what? We got our green cards. Imagine an American TV show starring a successful and elegant young lawyer and you will see Mr. Anderson. He told me he had followed his father and his grandfather into the profession. He was younger than I was and very intelligent. In the middle of my freedom struggle, I had found my good fortune.

I will never forget my first meeting with Mr. Anderson. He asked me, "Asya, do you understand the difference between a prenuptial agreement and a postnuptial agreement? This is an important question for you. It has serious long-term financial implications for you."

"Yes, I understand the difference," I said firmly.

"Then you must know that your husband's demand for a post-nuptial agreement that takes away your right to ask for any money or property is unreasonable. I cannot advise you to sign away your rights to community property. You were married for three years, and according to your financial statements, you contributed thousands of dollars to the household. In fact, it almost seems like he charged you rent. He has to compensate you for your contribution. This is not right," Mr. Anderson declared.

"I am sorry, Mr. Anderson. I am disappointing you. I know you want only what is best for me."

"Don't say sorry because I am hurt. Say sorry because you are going to get hurt."

"I don't know what hurts more," I said. "To fight for something he does not want to give or to leave without any support. If he would help, I would appreciate it. I am living by myself, taking care of my son, and I would be thankful for some assistance in this first period of my freedom. But if he doesn't offer me that help, I cannot ask for it."

"Why?" asked Mr. Anderson.

I could tell that he really wanted to know the source of my thinking. How could I not appreciate his patience? "Because he is the man, and a man should offer it."

"That's it?"

"Yes."

He waited like a therapist for me to say more, so I told him how Pavel had helped pay for my divorce from the Professor, had put a large downpayment on a house, had paid for the children and me to come to America, and had taken care of us before I started working. This investment would be normal for many husbands and all real lovers, but for Pavel, it was something special and we both knew it. I could not ask him for any more money. When I left him, I told him that he owed me nothing, and you can only imagine how quickly he agreed with me.

Mr. Anderson gave me more therapy looks. I said many more words than I have written here. The major idea was that Pavel had paid for my kids and me to come over here and start a new life, and it wasn't fair to ask for anything else.

"Asya, now I have a better understanding of you and this decision," he finally said.

"I am so glad to hear this from you," I replied. I thought to myself another of my many laws: don't ask for more than you have been given.

"Asya, you should know that this is quite unusual. I will be glad to help you go forward with this postnuptial agreement, but before this is over, we have to give Pavel a little bit of punishment for his arrogance."

True to his word, Mr. Anderson forced Pavel to pay a third of my legal fees. Though I was glad I hadn't demanded anything from Pavel, I was glad for Mr. Anderson's intervention. To me, it seemed only right.

Chapter Nineteen

The Spring That Did Not Come

Not everything that is shining is gold.

—Old Russian Saying

It was one of those late sunny afternoons in April that make you feel winter might be gone, though real spring had not yet arrived. Something flowed in the air and in my spirit that promised nature would soon be fully awake.

I was going on my first date in America, with an American man. Driving my old Ford Taurus, I listened to a light rock radio station, trying to sing with a "cool" voice. Don't laugh at me! I was a new student in the science of American dating, which had its own special rules and formulas. I learned that if the first date occurs in a coffee shop, it is meant for curiosity and evaluation. If a dinner date follows, it means an interest. No wonder I felt cool. An American man had skipped the curiosity step and gone directly to interest.

A feeling of incredible freedom surrounded me and gave me many wild thoughts. I can have a date or I cannot have a date. I can be a good girl or I can be a bad girl. I can stay with my date or I can walk away never to see him again and have not one stain of worry or guilt to clean off my soul. Yes, I was going out with a man I knew almost nothing about, except that his name was Brian (not his real name) and we had met in the parking lot of my apartment complex. I had put myself in a little intrigue, and I liked it.

For the first time ever, I was on my own without a man. Everybody in Michigan knows those December mornings when snow buries your car and you have to shovel tons of it to go to work. I think we got fifty centimeters that morning, almost two feet, and as I dug out, a man came next to me and began to do the same for his car.

We shoveled without talking, but when I couldn't get out of the parking spot and started to push my car, he offered to help. I returned the favor when he backed out his car and then we worked together to help someone else.

It was a cold fun. He told me that this adventure was not very typical for him because he lived in the south. He had come north for business and had stopped for one day to spend time with his old friend, who happened to live in our apartment complex.

I could feel a little sparkle between us. He asked me if I would meet him for coffee someday. I was in a good mood, feeling my freedom from all men. He was a tall man with gray hair and a beard and I liked the warm and smiling look in his brown eyes. Why not? I gave him my phone number.

Brian called the next day and said that he liked me and was serious about seeing me again. Unfortunately, he had to leave tomorrow, but in a few months he would return on business. He touched me with his deep, polite, and appreciative voice. In those three minutes, I heard more compliments than I had heard in the previous four years. Not surprisingly, his plan to impress me worked. I opened my eyes and my ears towards him.

Four months later he returned and asked me out for the dinner I was driving to when I started this chapter. What do I remember most about my first American date? The Italian restaurant? No, although I loved my pasta alfredo. The fact that he treated me? No, even though I was pleasantly surprised by his gentlemanly behavior. What I remember most was that Brian couldn't keep his eyes off me. I had almost forgotten the power of a man's admiring eyes. My adventure had given me something special beyond my expectations. Confidence surged into my personality. No, I didn't have a single thought about Pavel or the Professor.

Brian told me about his childhood in Michigan and his family and work in the south. He was divorced and had a son. I told him about my children and my challenges in adapting to American life. I didn't say much about my past. I didn't feel like touching it. Everything about the date was golden, until the end, when he asked me not to tell his old friend, the neighbor I did not even know, about our date. I heard the infamous click and knew this guy was afraid of somebody.

He returned to Michigan three months later. While away, he called me twice. In these conversations, there was no shortage of compliments about my looks or my personality. He assured me that I was often in his thoughts.

He asked me to come to his hotel restaurant for the second date. Yes, I knew that something would follow, and I was ready. I had not been romantic with a man for years. Naturally, my thoughts about him led me to intimate fantasies.

During the dinner, he was all smiles and warmth and filled me with his compliments and attraction for me. Then, from the farthest point of the universe, he kicked this hard ball at me.

"Asya, I have a girlfriend. Her name is Sally and we have been seeing each other for almost three years."

"Are you living together?"

"Yes, and we love each other. She is a terrific person and…"

I don't remember what he said next because I stopped listening. That's what he was afraid of, I thought. He didn't want his old friend at the apartment to tell Sally that he had sent some smiles to a woman who lived far way from her reaches.

Sally. Again there is another woman. Sally. Okay, it was absolutely normal for him to have this Sally, but it made a little sadness in me. Can I say to you Asya's latest law? Never trust a man. Oh, never mind, Dear Readers. This is not my law, just my frustration talking.

I thought of the Professor and his nose blowing and realized that Brian wanted to do this with me. Yes, I was now to be the third party. I was standing on the doorstep to becoming a bad girl.

I did not feel I was a bad girl in Italy. I deserved that light escape from the Professor's shadows, but now I would be the bad person.

Nonetheless, I decided to forgive myself for what I was going to do. I liked Brian. I felt relaxed with him. I knew what to do with my freedom, and I carefully landed on the earth.

"…I don't want to hurt Sally's feelings, but I want you so badly I can't help myself. Asya, you are very special. I have never met anyone like you before. I can't stop thinking about you. I even dream about you. One night I called your name and Sally woke up and asked me, 'Who are you calling? What is an *asya?*'"

"What a difficult explanation to make."

"It wasn't too bad. I got out of it quickly. She was too sleepy to care very much. She had never heard such a name, so probably it did not give her any images. But I must tell you that I love Sally. I have always been faithful, but my feelings for you are tearing me apart."

"Brian, I understand your feelings, and I don't want you to feel so unhappy and bad about yourself. It doesn't make sense. You have to stay with Sally and be happy with her. Your life is there. We are not going to make any stories or have a long-term relationship. I will never do that. But if this fire is burning you up, if you want me that much and can't help yourself, let's go to your room."

We finished our dinner without many words and walked with even fewer words to his room. I could feel his nerves. As for me, I felt peace. I knew it would be the first and last time with him, so I gave him what he wanted.

I needed nothing in return. He had given me more than I had asked for. I was grateful for his attention and his kind words. He helped me to feel like a woman again. What else could I wish for? When it was over, we said warm and friendly good-byes, and as I drove away, I felt a balance in me. But Dear Readers, I certainly was not singing any cool light rock songs as my car pushed into the Michigan night.

We never met again, but Brian roused the woman within me. She had been asleep since my trip to Italy with Pavel all those years before. The feeling of my deepest feminine energy came back. I could still be attractive. I could still be wanted. I could still be noticed. I could still give and receive. I could still manage my feelings. I could even gather Brian in and then let him go.

I could see Sally, his dear girlfriend, waiting for him, and I could put on her shoes. I didn't need to become Brian's queen; I could stay a lady. I knew how quickly a relationship could be tipped over a cliff, how easy it was to destroy love. I could live without Brian and not have a single desire to go back to him or continue our relationship. Thank God, he lived too far away for any serious drama. For me, everything was put in the right place in my heart, but one of my co-workers who had heard about this short romance as it unfolded cornered me at the office coffee pot.

"Is anything else going to happen with Brian?" she whispered.

"No." I was surprised that she would ask this private question with such directness. Frankly, I was a little amused. Why was she so concerned about my plans?

"Really? You are not going to fight for him?"

"Of course not," I replied.

"Aren't you worried about finding another man who cares for you as much as Brian did? You told me that he kept calling you."

"Yes, his heart caught a fire for me, but now it is put out. As long as I am open to love, it can happen again with another man, don't you think?"

"Asya, where does your faith in love come from? Haven't you been hurt a lot?"

"Relationships without a future are wrong. Maybe I could have Brian, but I would always know my happiness was built on someone else's unhappiness. We could never have a happy ending."

"You sound pretty certain."

"It is Asya's Law," I said with a smile and went back to my desk.

Chapter Twenty

Probuzhdeniye [7]

She looked at him, as one who awakens,
Her past was a sleep, and her life began.

—Robert Browning

Two years after Simon and I moved out of Pavel's home, Simon left for the university. I missed him terribly, but I was so proud of him. He graduated from high school with excellent grades and earned state grants. Without these grants, I had no chance of paying for his tuition. Despite all the twists and turns in his young life, he had a good attitude towards his future and a passion for computer science.

Anna and Jeff lived close by, but I tried to give them space to grow their relationship, as they had married. They were wonderful to me. Jeff, who was many years older than my daughter, owned two houses and let me rent one for next to nothing. Life was okay. I still had my job in the construction company as well as an evening job to help with the bills. As the Russians like to say, "After a rain comes fair weather." A little rain had come my way, but more sunshine was due.

---

[7] *Probuzhdeniye* means "awakening" in Russian.

One day, I was looking at my Yahoo email when I saw the word "Personals." I must have seen the word a thousand times. Now I asked myself, "What is that?" The word was attractive, and I thought maybe it would lead me to websites on personality development. I have to be honest; I didn't think too much about it. I was enjoying discovering new things about American life, and I clicked on it out of curiosity.

Next, I saw the phrase, "I am a woman, looking for a man." I was surprised but intrigued. I put in my age limits, 45 years to 65 years. I clicked for a search and found 420 men waiting for me. I was amazed that so many men were looking for women! What did they want? What were they looking for?

I started reading their profiles, looking at their pictures. I raced through some, but stopped on others and read them closely. I wondered about their lives, about their personal dramas. It reminded me of walking in the streets of Riga and saying to myself about men passing by:

I would never talk to that one.
That man probably beats his wife for small mistakes.
I would like to spend an hour alone with him!
Could we just have coffee together?

Maybe I was lonely, maybe I missed Simon, and maybe it was time to start something new. I am not sure, but I know one thing—I went to the computer more and more and scanned the personal ads. I wanted someone who lived no more than twenty-five miles from my house. Everything else was open to discussion except this: I did not want a man who thought he was perfect. I hated reading profiles like this:

I am smart, good-looking, in shape, a big picture thinker, loyal, dependable, sweet, sensitive, and of course sexy. I am a man's man but I love to laugh and appreciate the little things in life. I am looking for my equal, for a woman who will feel as comfortable in the bed as she does in the corner office, for that special woman without any problems and with a waist smaller than her hips and her top who can fully appreciate the pleasure that a caring, wonderful man can give. No drama queens, please.

Let this man find his perfect woman!

Out of the 420, I found one man I liked. His picture, a formal portrait, was the only black and white one. There were pictures of men with their dogs, in front of their cars, in wedding pictures with their wife's faces cut out, and with their shirts off in front of huge boats. Their things were more important than their personalities. Also, I didn't appreciate knowing so much about them before I met them.

I liked the formality and distance implied by the black and white picture. This man had a beard and eyes that saw into my soul. I imagined a man who would like the narrow streets of Riga. His profile contained no luxurious hints about his personality. The title of his profile was "Frustrated Writer Looking for Inspiration." I liked it. I had helped the Professor write his books. This man's only request was for a woman who understood how to raise teenagers.

I can do that, I thought. I asked Jeff what to do. He had given me good advice on many problems, like what car I should buy. I showed him the man's picture on the computer. "What do you think?" I asked.

"I haven't talked to him yet," Jeff replied.

He is so literal, I thought. "So, what should I do? Should I click on him?"

"I think you should stay in your home, be miserable, and not do anything," he said in mock seriousness.

His tone slapped me a little in the face. What did he mean? I wondered for a second, and then I understood his intention and made it much bigger and more liberating than his words or tone. It had been my choice to live with the Professor while he loved other women. It had been my choice to try to build a family with Pavel even when it looked impossible. It had been my choice to sleep with Brian. It was now my choice whether or not to contact Frustrated Writer.

I worked hard on that first email. I went back and forth from Frustrated Writer's profile to my email and debated whether to click

"Send" or not. In the email, I said that we had much in common—ages, birthdates, and children. Also, I said we were both interested in literature and the arts. I asked him if he wanted to continue the conversation. After two weeks of doubts, I clicked "Send."

Frustrated Writer responded quickly but with a surprise. *You must be mistaken. I did not write you a letter. Why did you write me?* I soon realized my mistake! In my email to him, I had called his profile a "letter" and said that I was responding to it. Americans did not think of their profile as a letter, even though, to me, it seemed like an open letter to anyone who read it.

Again, my poor English was haunting me. I had used the wrong word. I sent him an email, apologizing for my mistake, explaining that I was not an American. I told him that I was curious about him. Since we both lived in the same area, I asked him to have coffee. I thought it might be easier for me to talk than to write. He responded with a polite email that ignored my invitation for coffee and asked one question: "Why don't you have your profile and picture online?"

Now I felt embarrassed. Had I broken a rule? Was I too pushy? Could I have been any more stupid? People put pictures online to see each other before they met. Then I forgave myself. It was my first experience, and I would fix my mistake.

I had a scanner, but I didn't know how to use it. I called Anna, and she helped me through the software program. A few days later, I triumphantly wrote Frustrated Writer, announcing that my picture and profile would be online after approval from Yahoo Personals. Soon he would be able to make a decision about meeting me for coffee. A few days later, I got his reply.

"Your picture looks great. Let's meet for coffee." I laughed because the picture had worked so well. It reminded me of what had happened when Ivar saw me in my short skirt in Bulgaria. The tables had turned, and Frustrated Writer was asking me out.

We decided to meet on a Tuesday night at a local Starbucks. I got there first and planted myself in the middle of the café. I thought that Frustrated Writer would arrive in a long black coat with an artist's beard. Yes, he walked in wearing a nice black leather coat, but the beard was gone. I couldn't hide my surprise, and my first words to him were, "Where is your beard?"

"I shaved it off," he said.

Today I can only laugh at my question! We exchanged basic information about each other. I learned that he was a single father and the owner of a small business. He was trying to write a book to help his business. You could have packed my first impressions in a large trunk. He was smart, interesting, nervous, and filled with a lot of worries. He told me he had recently been to Europe and that he had loved it. He asked how I came to America.

I am not sure what happened inside of me when he asked this question. Certainly, I had heard it before. Was it the look in his eyes? Was it the spark of real interest in his question? I asked him if he really wanted to know. He told me that it was his profession to listen. I started talking and gave him chapter after chapter—from the end with Pavel to the beginning with the Professor. I kept going back, trying to explain the causes of my journey to America. After talking for twenty or thirty minutes without stopping, I realized what I was doing.

"Do I talk too much?" I asked him.

"You are not talking. You are telling a story."

He smiled, and I felt warm. I continued my story, until he said, "So you came here for love?"

"Yes," I admitted. We talked for a while longer, until he said he had to go. His son was waiting for him. We agreed to meet two weeks later at the same place and same time. I was so happy. I felt something nice and friendly in Frustrated Writer, and I forgot about his beard.

When he walked into Starbucks for our second date, he looked preoccupied, almost like he didn't want to be there. We started our conversation by sharing information about Yahoo Personals. I told him that I had received five or six emails in response to my picture. He asked me if I was seeing any of them, and I said that I wasn't. I asked him the same question.

"Yes, I am seeing about five women," he said.

"Oh, you must be very busy and very tired," I replied.

He laughed and shrugged his shoulders. "I don't see them all on the same night."

"I hope not." I thought about his situation and put myself in his shoes and spoke directly to the issue. "I understand that you are seeing other people. I like you. You are a very interesting person and I would be happy to be your friend."

"Good," he replied. Frustrated Writer smiled, and I saw him relax on the inside.

I wondered, what kind of troubles does he have with women? Don't worry, I thought. I won't be your sixth trouble.

We shifted the conversation to literature. He told me he had read Chekhov, Tolstoy, Dostoevsky, and Turgenev. I couldn't believe my ears. Frustrated Writer grew huge in my eyes. He was the first American I had met who had read Russian authors. He named the three Baltic nations and their capitals. (Lithuania, Vilnius; Estonia, Talin; Latvia, Riga.) Bonus points! He became irresistible to me.

Out of the blue, he asked me what I really wanted to do. I must admit that the Professor and I had shared a rich cultural life, but Pavel had never had any use for the nightlife. Whenever I'd asked him to go out, he had said, "I can listen to music at home."

I told Frustrated Writer that I wanted a man to share my cultural interests: jazz, foreign movies, blues bars, opera, theatre, symphonies, and to have good walks and talks. He seemed to absorb this information. Then, suddenly he jumped up, disappeared into the bathroom area, and returned with an announcement that he had to leave. I considered his actions a little abrupt, and I asked him, "Do you have to leave so quickly? Just like that?"

"Yes," he replied. "I have to go. I will call you. Here is my cell number in case you want to call me."

I appreciated his trust in giving me his phone number on the second date, and I didn't wonder if he would call me. If it didn't work, it didn't work. He was dating five other women, and if he made another choice, it was okay with me. I wasn't about to cook any tragedies. Nothing had happened yet.

I don't remember who called whom first, but I know that he asked me to a blues bar. I was flying. I had waited so long to hear live music. We ate a nice meal and listened to great music. We shared more and more stories. He had gotten a divorce after more than twenty years of marriage. I sensed that the break-up of his marriage had many tragic threads to pull and follow, but he didn't share them with me. He had a son and a daughter and seemed to worry about them constantly. His son lived with him, but his daughter lived with his ex-wife. He also told me that he wasn't really dating five women seriously. He had been involved with a younger woman for more than a year.

"Why are you doing the Yahoo Personals?" I asked.

"We agreed to date other people."

"Why?"

"We thought it might help us figure out how much we need each other."

This sounded strange to me. By agreeing to date other people, they had already agreed that they didn't need each other so much, but I didn't say anything. It meant a lot that he shared this deeper level of information with me. I began to feel even more friendly towards him, and I hoped he could straighten things out with his young woman.

For our next date, he asked me to a movie. I had only been to one movie in five years of living in the United States. He took me to see *Bowling for Columbine*. I knew the tragedy that had occurred at Columbine High School in Colorado, and I wanted to learn more about it. Frustrated Writer had an active interest in arts and politics, and his movie choice pleased me because he obviously wanted to share important ideas with me.

On the way to the movie, I met his son, as Frustrated Writer had to drop him off at basketball practice. A good-looking boy, he talked politely to his father and me. After dropping him off, Frustrated Writer told me, "My son likes you."

"He told you this?"

"Yes. It surprises me a bit. He doesn't usually like the women I date." I smiled to myself but was smart enough not to say anything more.

After the movie, we had dinner in another blues bar. Wow! Two concerts in less than a month! My life had really changed! As we sat eating, loud music forced us to write notes to each other to discuss the movie. We had both liked it, and it put us in a good mood. After dinner, we walked through the small suburban city, searching for coffee and dessert. It was early spring and a little chilly. He stuffed his hands in his pockets.

"Can I hang on you for a little bit?" I asked.

"Sure."

I linked my arm into his and leaned against him. I felt peaceful and safe.

We had now been on four dates, and you might think that I was planning a future with Frustrated Writer, but I refused to make any dreams about him. I breathed in the fresh air of a completely different man. In four dates, I had not heard a single click. He was a gentleman at every step, and no matter what happened to us, I already felt like I had achieved a lot. Was I continuing to look at Yahoo Personals? No, but I knew I could go back at any time.

The fifth date was magical. I waited for him in the restaurant, sitting at the bar. This situation was an adventure. To sit in a bar alone, smoking a cigarette, drinking coffee, waiting for a man, was something I had never done before. I enjoyed it. I felt free.

We had a great time. At dinner, he told me how much he loved his young woman. After my second glass of wine, I asked him, "Why don't you marry her?"

"I am not ready to marry her or anyone," he said. "But I would like to have a good relationship with her."

I could understand his thinking. I didn't want to get married again, but I was also seeking a good relationship. I have not told you this, but my Yahoo profile was titled "The Boat Needs a Sailor." My memories of Jurmala and the sea inspired this phrase. I can see now the powerful male and female symbolism in this title, but then, I just wanted to make an interesting profile.

After dinner, I had a surprise for him: a picture book of Riga. We went to Starbucks, sat outside, and I showed him my home. Every picture had a connection, an experience, a feeling, and I tried to share it all with him. He listened with great interest and asked me many questions about Latvia.

"Would you like to see Riga sometime?" I asked boldly, putting my face across the table.

"Yes, of course."

I felt his serious interest and it surprised me. When we finished looking at the pictures, he said he wanted to tell me something. I didn't know what was coming, but I was ready.

"Asya, I would like to introduce you to my circle of friends. I think they would really like you, and you would like them."

"Yes, of course! Thank you."

His face lit up and his eyes sparkled. "But, my girlfriend will also be there," he continued. "Will this be a problem for you? I have decided to stop this Yahoo Personal stuff and ask her to resume a committed relationship with me."

"It is absolutely fine with me. I would like to meet her."

He seemed happy with my response. He clearly liked me and wanted to keep a friendship with me. Immediately, I started imagining what I would wear, what pictures I would bring, and how I would meet his friends.

Now I know that my attitude towards his decision was very unusual. Most American women would be angry at a man who announced after five dates, all good, that he was returning to his girlfriend and, at the same time, inviting her into a serious friendship. But I wasn't angry. I was even happy. He had his life before he met me. Why couldn't he continue his life the way he wanted to? If he invited me to become a part of it, then it was an honor. Asya's Law: don't be cheap in friendship.

Usually, he called me a week or two weeks after we had a date, so I was surprised when he left me a phone message a couple of days later. I heard nothing but stress in his voice.

"Call me. I have broken up with my girlfriend." When I reached him on the phone, he was out of town and made it clear that he didn't want to talk about what had happened. I agreed to meet him on

Friday night. He took me to an Italian restaurant with great food and unforgettable wine. On the way to the restaurant, he again didn't want to talk about his girlfriend, but after a glass of wine he told me what had happened.

"I had lunch with my girlfriend on Wednesday. I told her that I wanted to resume a committed relationship and that I didn't want to date other women anymore. She readily agreed to this decision. Then I told her that I had met a really cool woman, you, Asya, and that I wanted her to meet you. I told her that you were from Europe and that I had been up-front with you about our relationship. Instead of welcoming the idea, she became furious. 'Do you expect me to believe this bullshit?' she asked. 'Either you drop her forever or you lose me.' 'Are you serious?' I replied. 'Yes.' 'Then, I drop you.'"

It was too much! Frustrated Writer was breaking up because of me! I had never caused a break-up before. I had never dated a married man. I did not fight for a man if he wanted another woman, even the Professor. I felt really confused. On the other hand, I was secretly proud that Frustrated Writer had chosen me, that, by himself, without any pleas, direction, or even hints from me, he had stood up to his young and pretty girlfriend. I could see that he was unhappy about this break-up and I wanted to support him, but as he told me the story of his relationship with her, I realized that breaking up was the right decision.

We drank more than we should have, and he asked me to drive home. Oh! I could do anything but that. He said, "You have to drive, baby. I am drunk."

He must be really drunk if he is calling me "baby," I thought. I hated so many things about this driving idea: darkness, unfamiliar roads, a strange car, and I was a little drunk myself. But I walked without any words to his car and started it. Thank God, he was sober enough to navigate. Of course I refused to take the freeways, in spite of his pleas, so we took the long way home. During the ride, he asked me a question.

"Why do you trust me after all that has been said and done?"

I had trouble answering him. The drive was so difficult, with my nose pressed up against the windshield, trying to see the strange roads. Finally I answered, "When I saw your picture, I said to myself, 'This is a person with destiny.' That is your part. As for my part, no matter what happens, I will never become a victim again."

Neither of us has ever forgotten that drive. We arrived home safely and I asked him inside.

Eight months later, we landed in Riga and started creating our own picture album of love. We are still working on it today, almost three years later.

Before I say good-bye to you, Dear Readers, I must tell you that while I can give you a recipe for borscht or for my favorite goulash, I can't give you one for love. I can only leave you with one more law: be free in love.

Asya's Borscht

Serves four to six

Put approximately one pound of soft and nice beef into a soup pot and add five quarts of cold water. Boil on a high fire and take off the foam with a regular spoon. Turn the fire to medium. Add salt and pepper and vegetables in the sequence suggested below:

- one whole medium white onion
- two medium beets sliced into long pieces that look like noodles
- two big carrots sliced
- one-half small cabbage sliced
- four medium potatoes cut into one-half-inch cubes
- one medium bell pepper sliced

Now, add four tablespoons of your favorite tomato sauce. I like ketchup! Add one teaspoon of sugar. Stir the soup, taste, and season with salt, pepper, or sugar to your satisfaction. Take a big sour Granny Smith apple and cut in halves and put both into the soup. Let the soup cook another ten minutes. Add three cloves of chopped garlic.

Remove the whole onion and what is left of the apples. Also, remove the meat and chop into small cubes and put back in the soup.

Now it is done! When serving borscht, you can offer sour cream and fresh chopped dill and/or parsley to give a wonderful flavor.

Asya's Goulash

Serves four to six

Cut two pounds of stewing beef into one-inch cubes. Fry the beef in small portions in a preheated pan. Don't fry all the meat together or it will lose its juice and taste. When fried to light brown, put the meat into a stew pot.

Fry one chopped medium-sized onion to golden brown and add salt and black pepper. Stir for a little while on a medium fire, then add two or three tablespoons of tomato sauce and one-half teaspoon of sugar. Stir slowly and add hot water to almost cover the meat. Turn the fire to low, put the lid on the pot, and let stew for about a half hour, stirring occasionally and adding water if necessary.

For additional flavor, add a sliced sweet bell pepper, a sliced carrot, and one or two cloves of chopped garlic. A stalk of parsley and/or dill won't hurt, and neither will a little sour cream. At the end of thirty minutes, taste the meat for softness.

Serve with mashed potatoes and fresh vegetable salad.

Good appetite!

If you enjoyed *Asya's Laws*, then read *The Search For Unrational Leadership*™ by Charles Fleetham

Midwest Book Review

The Search For Unrational Leadership: Using Rational & Irrational Methods To Change Your Life by Charles Fleetham (founder of Project Innovations, a management consulting firm serving business and government) outlines a strategy to create a "New Economy" based on the principles of what Fleetham has termed "Unrational Leadership." This refers to a process that Fleetham developed using both rational and irrational methodologies to solve complex problems and in the process, achieving some truly astonishing results in resolving societal problems without the side affect of unintended negative consequences. Challenging, unorthodox, at times iconoclastic, *The Search For Unrational Leadership* is nevertheless thoughtful, thought-provoking, stimulating reading that is especially commended to the attention of anyone having a managerial responsibility for problem solving within their businesses, their communities, their social causes and political/cultural concerns.

Available on Amazon.com and select bookstores